Minka

Minka
My Farmhouse in Japan

John Roderick

PRINCETON ARCHITECTURAL PRESS

NEW YORK

Published by
Princeton Architectural Press
37 East Seventh Street
New York, New York 10003

For a free catalog of books, call 1.800.722.6657.
Visit our website at www.papress.com.

Image credits
AP Photo: 250
Shizuo Kamabayashi/AP: 249b, 251t
Yoshihiro Takishita via AP: 99, 107
All other images courtesy of Yoshihiro Takishita

Editor: Dorothy Ball
Designer: Arnoud Verhaeghe

Special thanks to: Nettie Aljian, Sara Bader, Nicola Bednarek, Janet Behning,
Becca Casbon, Penny (Yuen Pik) Chu, Russell Fernandez, Pete Fitzpatrick,
Wendy Fuller, Jan Haux, Clare Jacobson, John King, Nancy Eklund Later,
Linda Lee, Laurie Manfra, Katharine Myers, Lauren Nelson Packard,
Jennifer Thompson, Paul Wagner, Joseph Weston, and Deb Wood of
Princeton Architectural Press —Kevin C. Lippert, publisher

Library of Congress Cataloging-in-Publication Data
Roderick, John.
  Minka : my farmhouse in Japan / John Roderick. — 1st ed.
     p. cm.
  ISBN-13: 978-1-56898-731-6 (alk. paper)
  ISBN-10: 1-56898-731-5 (alk. paper)
  1. Architecture, Domestic—Japan—Ise-shi. 2. Farmhouses—Japan—Ise-shi.
3. Vernacular architecture—Japan—Ise-shi. 4. Roderick, John—Homes and
haunts—Japan—Kamakura-shi. I. Title.
  NA7451.R63 2007
  728'.370952—dc22   2007015697

For Yochan and the Takishita family,
with all my love.

We shape our buildings, and afterwards our buildings shape us.

—WINSTON CHURCHILL

Contents

Prologue

When the hurly-burly of today's world overwhelms me with its
news of the never-ending war between good and evil, love and hate,
I hobnob with the rustic ghosts of centuries past in my restored old
farmhouse on a hill, overlooking Kamakura, the ancient capital of
Japan.

Its steep snow roof, massive posts and beams, wide wooden
floors, and split-bamboo ceilings take me back 273 years to the tiny
hamlet of rice farmers in the mountains where it was born, 350
miles from Kamakura.

The event on that distant day was a jubilant one because it
was built for the village chief, Tsunetoshi Nomura, who doubled
as its nature-worshipping Shinto priest. The place: Ise, in Fukui
prefecture, 400 miles west of Tokyo. Its scattering of farmers
all lived in such big farmhouses, called *minka*s, now a sadly
disappearing type of building more than 2,000 years old.

I became the owner of this venerable pile forty-two years
ago thanks to my surrogate Japanese family, the Takishitas (a name
meaning "under the waterfall") of Gifu prefecture. They took me,
an American journalist and recent wartime enemy, under their
wing in 1963, five years after I arrived in Tokyo to join the
Associated Press staff there.

Actually, the minka was a gift from its owner, Tsunemori
Nomura, the affable descendant of that long-ago ancestor for whom
it was built. Parting with it was, for him, an almost unbearable
sorrow. His ancestors, officers of a brave but doomed military clan
called the Heike, had hidden, lived, ministered, and died in Ise

since they had found refuge there following their twelfth-century defeat by Yoritomo, the first of Japan's long line of military rulers, called *shogun*.

What followed was a labor of love. The Takishitas, joined by friends and family, dismantled, moved, and rebuilt the immense old house in Kamakura, where I lived. After defeating the Heike, Yoritomo made Kamakura—his military headquarters—the capital of a united Japan. The ghosts of the Ise Nomuras must have laughed bitterly to see their old home come to life again in the seat of their ancient enemy. Yoshihiro, the youngest Takishita son, a recent university graduate, supervised the entire project. It took forty days.

In my forty years as a foreign correspondent, I covered the Chinese civil war, the strife surrounding the creation of Israel, and the French and American failures in Vietnam.

I spent seven months with the Chinese communist leader, Mao Tse-tung, in his 1940s cave capital of Yanan. And over the next thirty years, I chronicled the slow and sinister change in his personality from one of compassion for his fellow Chinese to blind hatred toward anyone blocking his dreams of personal power and conquest.

Turning from agrarian idealist to dictatorial tyrant, he publicly proclaimed that love was a bourgeois weakness, hate man's most powerful emotion. Yet I cannot believe him; I am still convinced that in the end the meek will inherit the earth.

Searching for an example of the power of love, I have drawn on my own experience, the Takishita family's gift of love and friendship whose living symbol is the old minka in which I still live.

It is a small example but it is significant because it happened in Japan, an implacable enemy that I—and so many Americans—once hated, intensely, blindly, and totally.

Often, in the eloquent silence of my high-ceilinged living room, I think I hear the voices of the Nomuras and their neighbors, chattering about the weather, the harvest, fishing, the hunt, the phases of the moon, and the religious mysteries of the deep forests.

It is then that the lovely old minka speaks to me of a time when nature and the rural sense of community sharing informed everyday life. Forty years after the Takishitas presented it to me, it is my private shelter from the global storms that rage all around us.

It represents, to me, the triumph of love over hate.

It is, at last, a house of my own.

Book One

The beautiful is that which cannot be changed except for the worse; a beautiful building is one to which nothing can be added and from which nothing can be taken away.

—LEON BATTISTA ALBERTI

A Breakfast to Remember

On the afternoon of Sunday December 7, 1941, I began to hate Japan and the Japanese, a nation and a race I hardly knew.

I was twenty-six then, the only editor on duty in the Portland, Maine, bureau of the Associated Press. It seemed like a quiet, eventless Sunday until the bells on our teletype machines began clanging, waking me from the daydream into which I had fallen.

The urgent message read:

JAPS BOMB PEARL HARBOR

The details came clattering over the teletypes: Carrier-based Imperial Japanese Navy bombers armed with torpedoes had, without warning, destroyed much of the U.S. fleet moored at Pearl Harbor on the Hawaiian island of Oahu. Eight battleships were sunk or severely damaged, 188 aircraft destroyed, 2,280 military men killed, and 1,109 wounded. Sixty-eight civilians also died.

The next day President Franklin D. Roosevelt described December 7 as "a date which will live in infamy" and congress declared war on Japan.

In the twenty-first century, the enemy is less visible, harder to pin down. He operates from secret headquarters and strikes at many targets hard to identify and defend. But there was no question about the enemy in 1941. It was Imperial Japan. A mixture of fact, fiction, and propaganda over the war years persuaded me, and millions of other Americans, that Japan was evil and the Japanese were monsters, buck-toothed, near-sighted, slow-witted, and cruel.

Inducted into the army in 1942, I studied the Japanese language at Yale University as part of a War Department program to train enough interpreters for the occupation of a defeated Japan.

My teachers, Japanese interned for the war's duration, were pleasant enough, but my revulsion persisted. The Bataan Death March in the Philippines, which took the lives of many American prisoners of war, and later atrocities increased my distaste for Japan and the Japanese.

When the war ended in 1945, I became an AP foreign correspondent in China. Becoming a foreign correspondent opened up a whole new, thrilling world for me. Within a month I was in Yanan living in a cave in the beleaguered capital of the Chinese communists and hobnobbing with their leader, Mao Tse-tung. I reported the harsh march of events that would lead to their conquest of all China in 1949.

From there I went to Amman, Transjordan, and reported the birth of Israel and the Arab world's attempt to stifle it in its cradle. Postwar London and Paris, my dream city, followed, and then French Indochina, reporting the French defeat at Dien Bien Phu.

In Saigon, I got an invitation in 1954 from a friend in Japan to visit Tokyo on my vacation. World War II had ended nine years before. I decided to accept.

I expected to find the city peopled with the cruel and unattractive stereotypes of wartime propaganda. I met instead a new generation of Japanese, embittered by the war their elders had foisted on their country and eager to learn about their American conquerors, who had conducted the military occupation firmly, which they expected, but also with compassion and intelligence, which they had not.

These Japanese were young, anti-war, and more pro-American than many Frenchmen I had known in Paris.

After years of hating the Japanese, I suddenly found them attractive, intelligent, and enthusiastic about democracy and its freedoms. Most young Japanese were sick and tired of militarism. They were eager to sample the privileges of democracy, to demonstrate and protest, which they did almost daily, without risking torture or imprisonment. Though they had little say in writing the American-sponsored "no war" constitution, they embraced it fervently. The roots of their pacifist credentials were visible in the destroyed cities and millions of war dead. Ashamed to be labeled pariahs, they yearned almost achingly to rejoin the family of civilized nations. I was willing to stop thinking of the Japanese as enemies and tentatively consider recognizing them as friends.

I talked to some diehard militarists, but they were few and no longer respected. They had nothing new or original to say; defeat had robbed them of their old, discredited, jingoist arguments.

Over the next five years, I returned to Japan on vacations from Paris and Hong Kong until, in 1959, AP gave me what I had once least wanted and now eagerly sought—assignment to Tokyo.

Besides admiring the defeated people, I found that I also liked Japan because in many ways it reminded me of China, where I had spent the first three years of my overseas career. In fact, I loved the Chinese and their culture so much I planned to end my career and retire in Beijing. When I lived there in 1947, it was a sleepy, dusty city of scholars, philosophers, and unfocused

dreamers. I felt I had the qualifications—it didn't take much—
to become one of those dreamers.

Mao, conqueror of China in 1949, shattered my plans.
Instead of acting like the poet he had been, he became an absolute
dictator, turned China into a nation of robots. He converted Beijing
into a noisy, busy, regimented metropolis as clunky and uninspired
as cold-war Moscow.

It was not what I wanted, so I said good-bye to my illusions
of a Chinese Shangri-La.

Over the centuries Japan, I found, had been influenced by
its giant neighbor. Wherever I turned, I saw Chinese influence in
Japanese religion, paintings, sculpture, literature, law, music, the
tea ceremony, flower arrangement, and government. Even the
ideographs of its language were borrowed from China. But the
Japanese made what they had taken peculiarly and markedly
their own.

Though I had loved China and the Chinese and had met
some congenial communists, such as its premier, Chou En-lai, I
chafed under the rigid controls and wrong-headed dogmatism of
the communist system. I was thrilled by the yeasty, noisy, freewheeling democracy of postwar Japan and glad to say and write
what I pleased without worrying what some communist bureaucrat
would think. Too many Americans, I thought, valued democracy
only when they lost it. To enjoy these freedoms alongside a culture
so closely resembling that of the ancient Chinese seemed more
than I deserved. It suited me down to the ground.

But what I had loved about the Japanese in 1959—their
relaxed way of life, willingness to talk endlessly about politics, art,
music, literature, the theater, and sex—by 1964 had been sacrificed
to the new god of industrialization.

The change was gradual. Almost from scratch, the Japanese began to rebuild their shattered economy. Those five years were devoted to rebuilding what before the war had been a booming industrial scene, and was now in ruins. When Tokyo was awarded the 1964 Olympic games, the rebuilding took off in a surge of relieved, grateful, and dedicated enthusiasm.

Yesterday's students graduated and began looking for work. Older Japanese with skills found more opportunities opening up with the rise of offices and factories. Those who had been demonstrating in the streets for political reforms found themselves preoccupied with new chances to earn money. A full rice bowl did much to change political perspectives.

The Japanese I had known abandoned me to join the huge work force in what I thought of as the same old rat race—the contest for industrial power and wealth, which I had hoped was a thing of the past. Others called it an economic miracle as the Japanese rose from the ashes of defeat to once again make Japan into a superpower. It was, I believed, a mistake. Life was simpler, and many people seemed happier in those pre-industrialization days than they had been before. As the race intensified, thousands of new factories spewed smoke into the air, spilled metallic poisons into the rivers and streams, and polluted the earth. In Tokyo in mid-afternoon one could barely see more than a few hundred yards into the distance.

Discouraged and disillusioned, I made plans to leave. Paris beckoned. The skies there were clear, the wine plentiful, the French preferred the good life to one based solely on material wealth.

In the midst of these preparations, I met a young Japanese man named Yoshihiro Takishita, familiarly known as "Yochan." He introduced me to his parents in his hometown, the Gifu mountain city of Shirotori, 350 miles from Tokyo. His father, Katoji, was a ramrod-straight ex–Imperial Army cavalryman, his mother, Kazu, a rosy-cheeked kimono maker still young-looking and energetic, was an amateur historian who regaled me with stories of the Gifu mountains.

They embraced me with an enthusiasm that astonished, then pleased me. It was the beginning of a relationship that has lasted more than forty years. The Takishitas have become my surrogate family, Yochan my adopted son. Because of them, our lives have changed and my long journey to Japan, which began in unreasoning hatred, has turned to love.

On subsequent visits I got to meet the farmers, carpenters, shopkeepers, *sake* brewers, timber workers, and small-town politicians of this rural city.

I saw that the backbone and resolve of Japan lay not in the seething big cities but in the enduring values of the villages: hard work, communal spirit, fatalism, love and respect for nature, superstition, religious fervor, and a refusal to admit defeat no matter what the odds they face. The industry and teamwork they foster and the natural skills they have mastered are the key elements of Japan's economic greatness. It is why, despite an almost total lack of natural resources, its economy now ranks second only to that of the United States.

When Yochan, witty, amusing, and optimistic, joined me in my rented house in Tokyo, I decided to stay in the country. Japan appealed to me not only as a good story but also as a place to live and work. Japanese culture and a newly acquired Japanese family, the Takishitas, were attractions I could not resist. There was something more: the Japanese themselves. Their pro-American friendliness and affection, honesty, sincerity, and unfailing courtesy I found refreshing. And their spare, clean, uncluttered lifestyle struck an answering chord. They seemed to be everything I wasn't and wanted to be.

Their extraordinary cultural accomplishments: folding-screen paintings, in which they excelled, the *kabuki* and *noh* theaters, calligraphy, woodblock prints, the many and colorful country and religious festivals fascinated me. And finally, and for me, importantly, their cuisine. Composed of the choicest natural ingredients, unchanged by few spices, served in an elegant setting, it was a new, and to me, exciting taste sensation.

All these things left a vivid impression on the small-city Maine boy that I was. They contributed to making me feel remarkably at home in this once-hated country.

After the Olympic Games, we moved to another rented house in Kamakura, on the coast thirty-five miles southwest of Tokyo. By this time, far from thinking of leaving, I began to envision the possibility of spending many more years in Japan.

The subject came up during breakfast one day. Our frisky little black dog, Hoagy Carmichael, frantically chased butterflies in the garden. The sun, rising red-faced over the distant bay, made me feel, like Voltaire's Candide, that all was for the best in this best of all possible worlds.

"What a beautiful place," I said to Yochan. "I wish I could buy a house like this, any house, in Japan. No more rent, no more nasty landladies."

It was idle talk, not to be taken seriously. In thirty years as an AP reporter and foreign correspondent, I owned nothing of real value and didn't want to. When tempted to do so, I remembered Thoreau's warning that we think we have things but, in fact, things have us.

Mine had been, until then, a carefree, rootless, vagabond life. With my new family, that was changing. I felt a responsibility in my dealings with the Takishitas, particularly Yochan, that I had never experienced before. He bridged the gap in our ages by treating me exactly as he did Katoji. They were more like brothers than father and son in the way they joked and played together, calling each other by their first names.

Quick-witted and ebullient, Yochan beguiled me with his boyish smile and bantering manner. But I had yet to discover that, like Katoji, once he made up his mind to do something, he was almost frighteningly unstoppable.

Yochan said nothing then but two months later, out of the blue, he asked: "John-san, did you really mean it when you said you'd like a house of your own in Japan?"

I paused. "Why yes," I replied. "But it was only wishful thinking. A dream, really. I don't have enough money."

He frowned. "Well, I took you seriously. My parents have found some old farmhouses, called *minkas*, not far from Shirotori. You might be able to buy one cheaply."

"No matter how cheap, I'm afraid I could not afford it," I replied.

Yochan shrugged.

"They've gone to a great deal of trouble," he said. "You could at least take a look at them."

Since we had met two years earlier, Yochan's family had been wonderfully kind to me. They had almost literally adopted me, a large American so recently an enemy, and at their insistence I had taken Yochan, their youngest son, under my wing during his student days.

Not that I needed any persuasion. From the beginning, despite the differences in our ages, race, and culture, we hit it off. At first I was *John-san*, the honorable John, but soon after it was just plain John, in the same way that he called his father and mother by their first names, something almost unheard of in relationships between Japanese parents and children. But Yochan was not an ordinary young man. For one thing he had an American sense of humor, an ability to laugh at himself, and a disdain for conventions. His relationship to his parents, and to me, could be described as affectionate, leavened with a large dose of bantering.

By the time Yochan mentioned the minkas to me I regarded the Takishitas as surrogate family. I loved them too much to do anything that might upset them. They had gone out of their way to find a house they thought I might afford. It would have been churlish to disillusion them, so I decided to play the game. The next day, Yochan and I met Katoji and Kazu in Shirotori, their hometown, spent the night there, and set out by taxi soon after breakfast for the remote hamlet of Ise.

Ise is in Fukui prefecture, an hour and a half from Shirotori, well off the main road that connects to the Gifu mountains. The area is wild and lonely, ideal for anyone seeking, for whatever reason, to hide from his fellow humans.

A monster of a house: the Nomura minka, Ise, 1965

Our taxi came to a halt before a cluster of about a dozen thatch-roofed farmhouses that, at first glance, seemed to have been battered in a recent battle. Six or seven were in various stages of destruction, roofs gone, walls crumbled, timbers sticking out like bones that had broken through their outer skins. There were vacant places where others had stood. Only six or seven had survived.

I looked at Yochan. He indicated he would explain later.

Silently, we walked through one house after another until we came to the one Kazu and Katoji liked best. It was a monster of a house. I had seen farmhouses in my native Maine and many in Europe. None was like this. Thirty feet high, its steep, thatched snow roof scowled down at me like an enraged elephant. Its size and height terrified me.

Out of the corner of my eye, I watched the reaction of the Takishitas, mère, père, et fils. Katoji and Kazu looked as though they were gazing on the newly discovered Egyptian tomb of King Tut. The rapture on their faces was reflected on Yochan's who, like me, was seeing it for the first time.

I wondered whether we were looking at the same house. We were.

When we stepped inside my wonder, and distaste, increased. It was cold, damp, cobwebby, dirty, and forbidding. I could barely discern through the gloom the immense posts and beams that held up the massive roof. My reluctant admiration at seeing these architectural wonders evaporated at the sight of the wide wooden planks that made up the floor. A floor like no other I had ever seen, it rose several feet in the air above a second floor of pounded dirt called a *doma*. The entire edifice was all too large, too strange, and too overpowering. It left me with a feeling of unease. Even if I could have afforded it—I assumed the price would be as high as its roof—this was not the house for me.

Though I plainly saw how they felt, I could not believe that the Takishitas seriously thought I would want such a monstrously big, obviously unheatable, and darkly repelling structure as my home. But, even as I reasoned that surely they were too sensible to harbor such ideas, I realized, with a pang, that they could and did.

I have always been sensitive to the feelings of others, a trait that borders on weakness. Because I loved them and understood their motives, I decided to remain silent while the Takishitas led me through this wildly improbable, never-dreamed-of, house-hunting nightmare. Out of politeness, I looked interested, but ultimately, and with a show of regret, I was determined to say no. Firmly.

The owner, a friendly, short, flush-faced, middle-aged man joined us a few minutes later.

"My name," he announced after bowing deeply, "is Nomura. You honor me by visiting my modest home. The house you are sitting in was built in 1734, and I am the head man of the village."

He looked at me and smiled.

"My ancestors were members of the Heike," he continued. "They built the first house on this spot in the twelfth century."

This bit of historical lore aroused me from my total lack of interest in the house-hunting proceedings. I had heard of the Heike. They were Japan's most celebrated losers. A military clan based in Osaka, they fought the Minamoto, based in Kamakura, for mastery of Japan in the twelfth century. After crushing them in a series of bloody battles, the Minamoto hunted them down almost to the last man. Few escaped. The Japanese see in their tragic end a sad commentary on the evanescence of life and a lesson in humility; even the most powerful must one day die and their works crumble into dust. The few descendants of the Heike enjoy a fame comparable to that of a home-run king or a movie star.

I looked at this small, meek-looking man with new respect.

"Even though I am an American, I have read about the Heike," I said. "They are well-known in Kamakura where I live. Your ancestors were brave and tragic people."

He bowed even more deeply.

"My honorable ancestor found safety here in 1188 after fleeing the victorious Minamoto in a famous battle," he said. "This house has many memories. And I hate to part with it. But that's fate. *Shikataga nai*. There's nothing I can do about it."

Katoji cleared his throat.

"It is kind of you to consider selling this stately home to John-san," he said, looking first at me, then at him.

"I would consider it an honor to give it to so famous an American journalist," he said. "I have been assured he loves and respects Japanese culture and that he will cherish it as his own."

I listened to this exchange in a daze, not quite sure about whom they were talking. Events were speeding up bewilderingly. I felt like a drowning man going down for the third and last time. I was losing control of the situation. This was not the scenario I had so confidently envisaged.

In this state of stunned confusion I heard Katoji's voice, faint and distant, saying to Nomura-san, "And how much, in your great and benevolent generosity, are you asking for this truly splendid house?"

The answer was short and to the point.

"Would 5,000 yen be alright?" Nomura-san asked.

This figure startled me out of my torpor. I am a numbskull at figures, but I knew that 5,000 yen in those days was the equivalent of fourteen U.S. dollars. I could hardly believe my ears. Hate it though I did, and though I didn't want it at any price, I recognized that his drafty but magnificent old house was worth considerably more than that.

Were these country people playing a joke on me, an innocent American? I didn't have time to ask. The Takishitas' faces lit up like sunrise over Mt. Fuji. Yochan beamed at me. Feeling foolish, I smiled weakly back.

Even after it had seeped into my consciousness that, instead of buying the old minka, I was being given it, my stunned mind refused to accept the fact. During what seemed an endless silence, I sat there saying nothing as all eyes were turned expectantly on me. Yochan made it clear I should accept.

Unwilling to make a scene but feeling foolish, I reached into my pocket and extracted the 5,000 yen—the price of a good lunch for one in Tokyo—and handed it to Nomura-san, who bowed yet again. The Takishitas applauded.

Briskly, Yochan produced a piece of paper and a pen and made out a rough bill of sale, which Nomura-san signed. Then a law student at Waseda University, this would be Yochan's first and last legal act. We didn't know it then, but the events of that day ended whatever youthful dreams he had had of being a lawyer.

I was now the reluctant owner of a huge minka I did not want, which I had acquired for a price I could not refuse.

"What in hell," I thought, "am I going to do with the damn thing?"

I smiled for the benefit of the Takishitas and Nomura-san. Anyone could have seen that I didn't mean it. But their euphoria was so great they thought it was the real thing.

Chaucer, Yochan, and Me

I was born September 15, 1914, in a three-story wooden house
on Western Avenue in the elm-shaded central Maine mill city of
Waterville. I might still be living there if my young, feckless father,
John Baptist, had not, two months after my birth, abandoned my
blond, blue-eyed mother, my four older brothers, and me.

Mother, after drying her tears, found a job in the local cotton
mill and my spinster aunt, Celia, undertook to raise this noisy,
lively brood of growing boys. She never liked my father. "Good
riddance to bad rubbish," she sniffed, after he disappeared into
the wilds of faraway Alaska. Aunt Celia bought the house, with its
wide, green lawns and glorious lilac bushes, and became our gruff
but indulgent surrogate mother.

Growing up in a crowded, noisy, permissive atmosphere, I
never missed my father. When he returned home in his coffin after
dying of heart disease in Hot Springs, Arkansas, I was sixteen and
writing news items for the local daily, the *Sentinel*. The story of his
return in death rated a two-column story on the second page.

Mother, mercifully, had died of cancer the year before.
Despite the family disapproval, she loved Father passionately—we
prayed every night for his return—until her last breath. They were
united again at last in the family grave, on the city outskirts, the
tears, misunderstandings, and anguish of their uncomprehending
lives finally ended. They were forty-nine.

Aunt Celia died the year I graduated from high school,
leaving the house to us. My part ownership was brief: My brother

Ernie persuaded me to exchange my share for his claim to land my father had bought in Muscle Shoals, Alabama, which proved worthless. Along with a new pair of Father's brown shoes, which fitted me perfectly, I inherited his wanderlust, love of adventure and, I am afraid, his poor financial judgment.

I became the *Sentinel*'s campus correspondent when I enrolled at Colby, the small Baptist college not far from our house, but after a promising start my grades began to suffer. College could not compete with the real-life education I got covering city hall politics, service club lunches, occasional murder stories, and midnight poker games with the reporters, printers, and press men of the paper.

A month before my scheduled graduation in 1936 I flunked Chaucer. My brother Ernie, in the same class, appealed to a wealthy member of the college's board of trustees for whom he worked part time, and after a makeup exam, I got my diploma along with the others who had really earned it.

Had I followed the advice of the head of the English department to do an extra semester, my life might well have been different. Six months after graduation the Associated Press hired me as a reporter in its Portland, Maine, office. I was its willing, and enthusiastic servant, in the United States and overseas, for the next forty-nine years, a career that might never have happened if I had done that extra semester at Colby.

After five years in Portland, I went to Washington, D.C., to cover the activities of New England members of congress. Six months later, the U.S. Army caught up with me and, after sending me to Yale to study Japanese, loaned me to the Office of Strategic Services (OSS), the wartime predecessor of the Central Intelligence

Agency. Wasting no time, the OSS moved me to west China where, aside from a brief stint interpreting for French-speaking soldiers from Indochina, I served with no particular distinction.

I rejoined the Associated Press as a foreign correspondent in China at war's end and a month later accompanied three other reporters to Yanan, the Chinese communist capital next to the Gobi Desert. It was the first postwar visit permitted to the cave city, which the nationalists of Chiang Kai-shek had for a decade encircled and barricaded. My joy was unbounded; it was an assignment most veteran correspondents would have given their eyeteeth to get, rubbing shoulders with Chairman Mao Tse-tung and the leaders who, after 1949, would rule all of China.

I reported from Yanan, Beijing, Shanghai, Nanking, Manchuria, and the borders of Tibet for the next three years and by that time had fallen in love with this vast country and its fascinating people. So much so, I planned to spend the next three years in France, the home of my ancestors, and, after sampling its widely known pleasures of the body and mind, return to Beijing. I hoped to while away the rest of an indulgent, misspent life there in the shadow of the Forbidden City, contemplating my navel.

The AP in New York put my application for a Paris assignment under the "Ps" in its personnel files and, in due course, advised me I had been chosen to go to Palestine, an unfortunate alphabetical mistake, I thought, but one I was unable to correct.

From Palestine, and its ancient religious and political hatreds, I moved to London, then lived five gratifying, sybaritic years in Paris, proving that good things come to those who wait. After two years reporting the defeat of the French in Indochina, another two in Hong Kong, where I resumed writing about China, from a distance, and a seven-month return visit to Paris, I finally arrived in Tokyo in 1959.

Now, in my old age, I look back in gratitude at the talented humans who, over the centuries, have created the art, architecture, music, and literature that have enriched the lives of those of us who have been lucky enough to know and enjoy them. Without unusual creative talent myself, I am indebted to those people, now and then, who have made existence for me, and countless millions, meaningful and rewarding. I count among these benefactors the Takishitas of Gifu, who found the graceful old minka that has played such a thrilling role in my life.

During the first twenty years of my time as a foreign correspondent I lived in a variety of shelters, some flea bags, others luxury apartments, all interesting, in such far-flung places as China, Hong Kong, the Middle East, England, France, North Africa, and Indochina. My landlord in Paris was an eccentric French baron; unlike the majority of his countrymen at the time, he liked Americans, so the rent for five elegant rooms was cheap— $125 a month. In Peking, then called Peiping, and later, Beijing, my host was another Frenchman, a genial 75-year-old surgeon with blue eyes, a cherubic face, and a cellar of admirable French wines. The rent: $35 a month, including six servants. Mao Tse-tung offered to pick up the tab for my seven months in the caves of the American Dixie Mission in Yanan. Even though Senator Joseph McCarthy had not yet embarked on his redbaiting witch hunt in Washington, I knew that the word "communist" spelled trouble and paid the stiff-backed American commanding officer instead.

The thing all these dwellings had in common was that they were rented. I was on the move too much to even think of buying one. And besides, what could I possibly do with a used communist cave?

After I met the Takishitas in 1963, Yochan and I and our dog Hoagy moved to Kamakura because my Tokyo landlord refused to alleviate the punishing heat of summer by replacing the tin roof of my tiny house with something cooler. The Kamakura house seemed like a dream come true. It looked out on a green valley and the distant bay. Hoagy—her earlier Japanese owner loved Carmichael's music—reveled in the high grass, thick woods, and wide-open spaces.

I could have spent the rest of my life there and I might well have had I kept my mouth shut during that fateful breakfast. But I am a creature of impulse, and if it hadn't been then I suppose it could have happened later. Let's say that fate intervened.

In the relatively prosperous Japan of today, large houses are fairly common. But in the 1960s most Japanese people skated on the thin ice of survival. Tokyo was so crowded even a modest house was too expensive to build and impossible to find. I knew a bank manager who thought himself lucky to live in an *apato* barely big enough for him and his wife to lie down in. He had to use a communal toilet, bathed in a public bath, and, lacking cooking facilities, ate out every day.

There were several reasons why I hesitated to accept the Nomura minka. One of these was my parlous financial situation. And no bank at that time would loan money to a foreigner, certainly not to a less-than-affluent American journalist. The size of the thing also gave me pause. It fitted neatly into the countryside next to its equally huge neighbors, but I could think of no place in Kamakura, or almost anywhere else, big enough to accommodate it gracefully. I envisioned it rising somewhere on a narrow street, dwarfing the buildings around it, a source of wonder, terror, and resentment to those around it.

None of these considerations apparently weighed on the minds of Yochan or his parents. To them, living in a minka seemed perfectly normal. All the Takishitas were born in one. Before the war no one in the country lived in anything else.

I accepted the self-evident fact that without enough money, I couldn't own land or build a house in Japan. The Takishitas thought otherwise. They were guided by gut feeling, what is called *haragei*. Their instinct, fortified by years of tough mountain existence, told them that anything was possible if you put your mind to it. Besides, John-san wanted a home of his own in Japan. And what John-san wanted, John-san got. It was as simple as that.

A mystery in a swimming pool brought Yochan and me together in the very hot summer of 1963.

It wasn't only the heat that bothered me. For months I had become progressively disillusioned with life in Japan. In 1954 the pace of life was slow, and people had time to sit in the coffee houses and talk, endlessly, about music, art, and the future. By 1960 all this had begun to change. American policy makers, watching the triumph of Mao Tse-tung and communism in China, believed that a strong, re-armed, industrialized Japan could become a valuable ally in the Cold War against Soviet and Chinese communism. Their pent-up energies released, the Japanese responded with enthusiasm. But in the headlong rush to modernize, they darkened the skies, muddied the waters, and poisoned the land with the pollutant offshoots of a hundred thousand new factories.

My friends no longer had time to talk or otherwise savor life. They were too busy working around the clock making money. You couldn't blame them; they had had so little of it before. Since there seemed little difference between it and Los Angeles, New York, or Buffalo, I thought seriously of leaving Tokyo and going back to Paris where the food was superb, the wine excellent, the skies clear, and the French ready at the drop of an escargot to dispute anything you had to say.

It was then that Yochan and the Takishitas helped me discover rural Japan, one I could live with.

I had gone to the old outdoor Olympic swimming pool in Tokyo for relief. Independently, so had Yochan. A gaggle of screaming, yelling, boisterous children was ahead of us. They filled the pool, making it impossible for us to use it.

On the way out, I paused to peer into a smaller pool, on whose bottom rested an entirely submerged Western-style living room: tables, chairs, even a television set. Yochan was standing beside me.

"*Nan desu ka*?" I asked. "What is it?"

"*Mezurashii desu ne*," he replied, scratching his head. Then in English: "It's strange isn't it?"

We smiled at each other. Of medium height, he had the slender body of the champion high school swimmer he had been, an open, friendly face, an engaging grin, and a manner so innocent of guile it encouraged strangers to speak to him.

Fresh from the country, he had never known an American except the Occupation soldiers of his childhood who doled out chocolate bars and chewing gum to him and his older brother, Katsumi, part of a rag-tag army of wandering Japanese children intrigued by these large, white, blue-eyed aliens so strange they could have come from outer space.

In the presence of the minor mystery of the small pool—
we never figured out what it was—Yochan and I acted as though
we had known each other for years. We felt comfortable together.

"*Gakusei desu ka?*" I asked. "Are you a student?"

"Yes," he replied. "I'm studying law but I really want to learn
English."

During my nine years in Japan I had heard this before. But
there was such an earnestness in the way he said it, I decided he
really did.

We introduced ourselves, exchanged addresses, and promised to
meet again.

A month later, I went to Shirotori, which means "white bird,"
and met Yochan's father and his mother. Shirotori, like Waterville
in central Maine, where I was born, lies on the bank of a river.
Mine is the Kennebec, theirs the Nagara. Benedict Arnold made
the Kennebec famous when, while still loyal to the American
revolutionaries, he sailed up part of it to attack Quebec. The Nagara
is known for its ancient cormorant fishing festival at Gifu city.

The two cities have populations of about 15,000 each.
Waterville is a mill town that boasts the small college where I
studied, Colby. It is on the main highway to French Canada.
Shirotori also has mills, mostly timber, and it is on the way to
the Japan Sea coast. But it has no high school, let alone a college.
Yochan had to commute to Gifu city, three hours away, to complete
his secondary education.

The Takishitas moved to a modern wooden house in
Shirotori from a minka in the nearby hamlet of Nakatsuya when
Katoji became the number-two man in the rural cooperative. This
house has floors of straw matting called *tatami*, unheard of in

Waterville. The Takishitas sleep on mattresses called *futon* that they lay on the floor and fold away during the day. Waterville's houses also are made of wood but are larger and more busily furnished. They have well-tended lawns and back-yard gardens.

Christian churches and synagogues illustrate Waterville's religious preferences. In Shirotori the temples and shrines of worship are Buddhist and Shinto. There are no Christian churches or synagogues and few, if any, Christians or Jews. Yet the attitude there, as elsewhere in Japan, is tolerant toward religion. Though they are small in number, Christians are accepted and some of them rise to impressive political heights. This was not always so. From 1615 to 1868, under the military shoguns, Christianity was banned, its followers executed.

The Japanese, particularly in the countryside, are deeply devout. Every house that can afford it has a large finely carved, ornately gilded Buddhist altar as well as a smaller, more modest Shinto shrine. There are religious festivals at New Year's, called *Shogatsu*, and a summer festival for the dead, known as *Obon*. Street dances and elaborate ceremonies involving portable altars carried by increasingly inebriated young disciples are highlights of other celebrations. I have never seen anything like it in Waterville.

Though there are flowers and small gardens everywhere, the people of Shirotori live closely together, leaving little room for spacious lawns. The Takishita house and its neighbors would seem to an American embarrassingly close. But the Japanese have long ago come to grips with this dilemma. They refuse to see what they do not want to see. The Japanese are not voyeurs, and because no one is looking they do not feel constrained to draw the curtains.

If the place and the customs differ widely from what I have been used to, the people of rural Japan are even more strikingly different. Though I found them less reserved than those of the cities, with whom I am more familiar, they nonetheless kept their distance and did not encourage easy intimacy.

As an American of Latin origins, I tend to be outgoing and sometimes impetuous in expressing myself. The Takishitas avoid physical closeness. They bow when introduced, smile to show their appreciation, and occasionally shed a tear when the occasion calls for it. Later, after I succeeded in knowing them better, they displayed emotional stress they otherwise would have hidden from a stranger. But no matter how happy the event, hugging or other friendly bodily contacts such as ritual kissing on the cheek, which Americans practice routinely, are frowned on.

I mention these differences to emphasize the difficulties attendant on my increasingly warm relationship to the Takishitas. Not only did we not share the same culture, religion, or global outlook, we did not speak the same language. They did not know a word of English and my Japanese, learned twenty years before at Yale, was minimal. Yochan, still mastering English, stepped into this breach. Through him Kazu and Katoji made their feelings known and learned of mine. They said that in the month or so since we had met in Tokyo, Yochan had talked so much, and so warmly, about me that they felt they already knew me.

For 250 years, until it was pried open by the United States in 1853, Japan walled itself off from what it regarded as the hostile elements of the outside world. A century later, the Japanese still looked on Westerners as interesting barbarians, but barbarians nonetheless. The military occupation dispelled some of their deep-seated fears, but Americans remained a hard-to-understand, highly mixed race.

Yet despite these differences of culture, language, and race, or perhaps because of their affection for Yochan, Kazu, Katoji, and I got on famously from the moment we were introduced. Katoji told me of his war experience in China in 1938, three years before Pearl Harbor. The food was poor, and he came down with malaria. Transferred from the south to Shanghai, he elected to go there on horseback. The rest of his company, many of them from Shirotori, went by ship. It was sunk en route. There were no survivors.

Returning to Gifu, he worked the family rice fields and later got a job in the rural cooperative, called *nokyo*. As a youth, he had wooed the beautiful girl across the river. It was a hopeless pursuit. She was already engaged to another. He married her sister, Kazu, instead.

A remarkably lively woman, Kazu remembered the hardships of the war, when meat was available only once a year. To keep her small family alive, she made kimonos and went from house to house in the area selling them.

"It was hard, exhausting work," she recalled. "I had no transportation, had to carry the heavy kimonos on foot in a bundle tied around my neck."

An amateur historian, she told me of the facts and legends of the Gifu mountains, some of which I will relate later.

Darkly handsome, his body as lean as when he was a cavalryman, Katoji talked little but knew a great deal. He spoke knowledgeably about current events, including international affairs, and was unusually familiar with American issues and problems. He asked informed questions on subjects that interested him. I found this astonishing since he had not gone to college; Yochan was the family's first university student. When I asked him about this, Katoji said the *Asahi* newspaper and publicly supported television, both available in Shirotori, kept him up to date.

Few Japanese I met then, or afterward, talked of the war. Katoji and I did partly because we each had served in China.

"War is stupid," he said, "and this one was a mistake. We were taken in by the militarists, looked on Americans as devils. I suppose you had the same idea about us. The fact that Japan and the United States now are allies and that you and I are friends shows how stupid and unnecessary the war was."

Katoji and Kazu begged me to look after Yochan on my very first visit to Shirotori. They plied me with gifts, many so valuable I hesitated to receive them. Hardly a week passes, even now, without the arrival of homemade pickles, wild mushrooms, other mountain herbs and vegetables, or some old curio from the country.

Despite all these evidences of affection, I found it difficult from the beginning to overcome the deep-seated hatreds bred in me by the war and its cruelties. The Takishitas offered me not only friendship but a place beside their sacred family shrine. This might not seem so unusual in America where intimate relationships are easily arrived at, easily broken. But Japan is a devout, highly structured society that emphasizes loyalty, obedience, and, above all, conformity. If I accepted, it would mean the end of my freewheeling, carefree bachelor existence. I would have responsibilities, never very onerous but serious nonetheless, to my new family, especially to Yochan during his student days, and maybe thereafter.

I knew I would be committed, not for a year or a season, but for life.

Year of the Tiger

I often think back, sometimes wryly, sometimes with a laugh, to the hours after I had been stampeded into "buying" the Nomura minka. I felt like a boxer who, for the smallest fraction of a second, looks right when he should have looked left. Still dazed from the blow, I began to think disloyal thoughts about the Takishitas. Had they colluded with Nomura? Why was he so willing to part with his ancestral home for a measly 5,000 yen? And to a foreigner, at that. I suspected the Takishitas had secretly bought it and given it to me because they felt an obligation to gratify my wish to own a home of my own. In Japan one mustn't admire anything too lavishly; your host will end up giving it to you.

There was an awkward silence as we left Ise for Shirotori. "Why only 5,000 yen?" I asked.

"The fact is," said Katoji, "the village is soon to be flooded by the new Kuzuru River Dam reservoir. The dam authority, reacting to newspaper criticism, has ordered these minkas removed."

"We told Mr. Nomura you were looking for a house, that you were reliable and would cherish it. More importantly, we said, and I hope you agree to this, that you would pay to take it down and move it."

Yochan chimed in. "He is happy his old home will be reborn and lived in again. He is grateful to you."

I now understood that there was little I could do about it. Forces had been set in motion, like the general mobilization of the Imperial German Army on the eve of World War I, which could not be halted. I still hoped, rather vainly, that the Takishitas eventually

Disassembled and about to be trucked from Shirotori to Kamakura

would see as I did that the whole adventure was impractical and undoable. The problem was that they talked to me in polite circumlocutions. I, wanting to be just as polite, did the same. We were ships, lights doused, passing each other in the night.

Given this state of partial, or total, non-communication, I was paralyzed, uncertain what to do. When Yochan asked me to give the order to begin the dismantling process, I numbly agreed.

A few days later, Katoji and a Shirotori city councilman we shall call Tanaka, arrived in Ise to take the minka down. The team they directed, warned that it was destined for a life after death, pulled it apart with great care and delicacy. Blackened and hardened with age, the ropes holding together the massive roof beams had to be cut with axes.

Tanaka had taken down forty of these country behemoths and put them back together again, usually close by. All continued to serve as less-than-satisfactory farm homes, their owners just as unhappy as I at their size, cold, and disease-breeding dampness. He had never moved a minka for a foreigner and was astonished that I intended to live in it. Couldn't I afford something better? Weren't all Americans rich?

Clouds of dust rising from the centuries-old thatch as it was torn from the roof guided Yochan and me back to the site as work began. It looked like a distress signal sent up by some primitive tribe. Katoji and Tanaka wore handkerchiefs over the nose and mouth to keep from choking.

I felt almost embarrassed as I watched the workers picking apart what had earlier seemed to me a terrifying beast, a shaggy mastodon from the past. As they stripped away the old thatch the minka's great, raw-boned skeleton came to light, reducing it from a thing of awesome grandeur to one helpless and naked. Once it had become an orderly pile of timber on the ground, I felt personally cheated. There no longer was anything to tilt my lance against. Laid out in this way, it had no fight left, no personality, no élan vital. I was awakened from this quixotic daydream by Katoji thrusting an old wooden panel into my face, a relic of the only so recently living minka. He had found it concealed at the top of a display niche called a *tokonoma*. Turning it over, he found a *tanka* poem on the inside that read:

> Columns of frost
> Beams of ice
> Roof beams of snow
> This house is the repository
> Of the Sacred Tree.
> —*Erected in the Year of the Tiger, the Nineteenth of Kyoho*

The poem had remained hidden, an integral part of the minka, for more than two centuries, waiting for the inevitable day when, on dismantling, it would be discovered and yield its secret, the exact date of its construction, 1734, information usually lacking about these old Japanese houses.

This dedicatory poem not only disclosed its age but confirmed the high religious and civic status of the Nomuras in the hamlet; Katoji said the "Sacred Tree" referred to the *sakaki* whose branches are used in Shinto ceremonies.

The first lines of the poem are an elaborate attempt to deceive the god of fire. Since it is made of frost, ice, and snow, the god would waste his time trying to burn it down. As the resting place of the sacred sakaki tree, to persist would add sacrilege to folly.

Nomura gave me a heavy wooden mask of the fire god so fierce and frightening it was immediately understandable why the good citizens of Ise nourished such a fear of him. When, with an air of gravity, he then handed me an old wooden box containing a frayed silk blouse and the stiff, black lacquered hat that were symbols for centuries of the Nomura family's spiritual ascendancy, I was deeply moved. I recognized that I had acquired not only a house but a spiritual center steeped in the human and religious memories of ages. With this gesture, Nomura acknowledged the end of an era for his family. His next home would be the small modern house near Nagoya that, with the government's help and my contribution, he was able to buy.

The long-hidden poem revealed that the Ise villagers lived in a fortunate time, during the reign of an able and compassionate military ruler, the shogun Yoshimune. Unlike many of the other shoguns of the Tokugawa period, who were tyrants, he was fair and honest, consulted his subjects on many matters, and avoided cruel and unusual punishments. Before and after his time, the military *samurai* class had the power of life and death. Armed with two swords, these arrogant retainers of the higher lords could with impunity strike off a commoner's head at some real or imagined slight. Ordinary people had no rights, were not even entitled to a family name. Under these circumstances, Yoshimune's magnanimity was even more remarkable.

But by 1754 he was dead, and his successor, weak-minded and ignorant, made a show of continuing Yoshimune's practice of receiving petitions from the common people. To discourage its too-frequent use, he lopped off the heads of the first two or three signers, usually village chiefs.

At that time, the Takishita ancestors, known solely as the Sakubei—peasants weren't allowed to use family names until 1868—lived in the village of Nakatsuya, not far from Shirotori. In 1775 they signed, along with thirty other rice farmers, a petition to the shogun against the harsh rule of the governor. They must have been desperate to take so dangerous a step.

The addle-pated shogun was not amused. He granted the petition, removed the governor, and had all thirty-two of the signers executed. Yochan's two ancestors were among them. Recently, we journeyed to the spot to see the new granite monument that tells their story.

It took ten days to take down the Nomura minka and truck it to Shirotori, where it was stored in a hastily built shed on the abandoned high school yard. It had cost $2,000 of my meager savings, but I was prepared to pay cheerfully if that was the end of the adventure. It wasn't.

In the weeks after this, Kazu and Katoji came to Kamakura to reassure me about the magnificent acquisition I had made. They told me the history of minkas. Before the modern period, nearly all Japanese lived in them. The city ones were more fragile and had more elegance, their rough beams concealed by a thin wooden ceiling. Instead of dirt domas there were straw floor coverings, tatami, now found even in rural minkas.

Today one can still see minkas dotting the countryside but they have almost totally disappeared from the cities, replaced by less attractive and distinctive modern Western houses.

Fire, earthquake, floods, and neglect have taken their toll on minkas in the rural areas. But the real enemy is growing farm prosperity. More and more farmers are selling their land at un-dreamt-of prices, leaving behind their family minkas for the new owners who tear them down and put up something modern and full of gadgets in their place. The lucky farmers take the money, put up more livable modern houses of their own, and sock the rest into the bank. They can be seen all over America and Europe these days riding the trains in their underwear, gaping at the Empire State Building or admiring the *Mona Lisa.*

I knew that farmers, fishermen, artisans, merchants, and handicraftsmen lived in these old houses. But I hadn't heard that foreign journalists did. I was determined that this one never would.

It didn't seem fair to me that I should be chosen to stem this lamentable but inexorable decline of the minka. At the same time, my unexpected ownership of the Nomura minka prodded me into some idle thinking about the age into which it was born. It was an era, as I have said, of rare good government by the shogun, one of many military dictators who kept Japan under their harsh thumbs for 800 years. My ancestors in France were under King Louis XV, but in a little more than thirty years they would be caught up in the French Revolution, which led to democracy. The Nomuras would have to wait another 140 years for anything comparable to happen.

It was all very interesting, I thought, but hardly germane. There would be no Roderick minka to dream about.

The Great Peak

I didn't hear a word from Shirotori all winter. This silence bred in me a sense of false security, rather like the months of inaction that followed the outbreak of war in Europe in 1939. Could Kazu and Katoji have forgotten about the Nomura minka? I didn't dare raise the subject with Yochan, and he also remained silent.

This state of affairs lasted until the ground thawed and the first buds cautiously appeared on the plum trees. Spring sets the juices running not only in nature but in humans: after a long winter of hibernation, they stretch their legs, cast an eye on their surroundings, and decide they should look for new places to live. The Takishitas went through this process. But instead of thinking about a new home for themselves, they thought of one for me. The phone began to ring in Kamakura without letup. The message was clear and unequivocal.

"Spring has come," they told Yochan. "It is the best time of year to look for land."

Aware of my reluctance, Yochan said, "Think of it as a lark. A chance to see some of Japan."

Put that way, I agreed. I was convinced we never would find a piece of land that would fit my pocketbook. Getting the minka for nothing was a fluke. It couldn't happen again.

We enlisted the help of a group I had never met before, the real estate salesman, or *fudosanya-san*. In Kamakura, they sat in broom-closet-size offices, their windows advertising land at astronomical prices.

In a country where land prices are so high, those who deal in real estate stand to make handsome profits. There is an understandable tendency to gild the lily in describing what is available; the Japanese fudosanya, however, in their dealings with us did not merely embellish the truth, they lied. We were shown plots "near the station" that were miles away, others with a "view" if one jumped high enough, and many with non-existent water, electricity, telephone service, or other utilities. Some plots were difficult or impossible to reach. At least no one tried to dupe us into putting a deposit down on land that wasn't for sale, others weighed down with towering unrevealed mortgages, or plots on which buildings were forbidden. These things happened to many less-wary people.

I rather enjoyed these weekend searches. The disappointments buoyed my secret hope that nothing would be found, and the minka project would have to be abandoned. Yochan turned out to be a cheerful, light-hearted traveling companion.

Then one day I met up with an old friend, "Shamisen" Yuchan, so-called because he was a professional player of that traditional stringed instrument. Temporarily unemployed, he worked for a Tokyo real estate firm and introduced me to its Kamakura branch. It had two sedan cars at its disposal and drove us to an East Kamakura area of neatly laid out parcels of land, complete with utilities and paved roads. Called *danchi*, they would be crowded in a few months with new Japanese urban dwellers.

"Tell them," I said to Yochan, "they are quite splendid but too small for a large minka. It needs a wooded hill, a field of wild flowers. It would be as out of place here as a skyscraper."

The fudosanya, apparently annoyed that this difficult

foreigner didn't appreciate their efforts—we had seen a dozen danchis—conferred with his colleagues.

"Well," he said, "we have something on the other side of Kamakura. But it is not suitable. You won't like it."

The sun had begun to set as we rolled through a tunnel in the residential area west of Kamakura station and headed up a steep dirt road past a Shinto shrine. Sweeping under a canopy of trees in an unfamiliar park, we emerged onto an uninhabited hill covered with tall grass and a few trees. The city of Kamakura lay below us, the sea glinting under the rays of the fading sun.

We felt faint. It was everything we had been looking for and hadn't found.

It now seems improbable, but at that moment I thought of Keats, and his poem about Cortez discovering the Pacific:

> And all his men
> Look'd at each other with a wild surmise—
> Silent, upon a peak in Darien.

That was how Yochan and I felt on our hill—it is called *Omine*, or "Great Peak"—as we gazed down on the bay. One lot at the top of the hill commanded an unobstructed 180-degree view. That was the one we wanted.

It would be difficult to describe the elation I felt as we clambered up the worn stone steps and wandered around this piece of land crowning the bare hill. Until then my interest in building a house in Japan had been minimal. I hadn't dreamt I would find land with such a commanding view. I exulted at the thought, carefully withheld from Yochan, that I could build anything on such a magnificent site and feel like a king, or a shogun, or an emperor. It didn't have to be a minka. A shack or a tent, or just possibly a small, neat, affordable log cabin, would do. Suddenly I became land crazy, totally, desperately, unrequitedly in love with this quarter of an acre. I decided that, no matter what, I must have it.

My euphoria soared to dizzy heights. Then the fudosanya brought me crashing down to earth.

"This is not for sale," he said. "The only one actually available is down there."

We tramped down to a plot fifty yards southwest on the north side of the dirt road. If one squinted a bit there was a view of sorts. I felt like crying.

"Don't give up," said Yochan. "This at least is better than anything we have seen so far."

"How much?" I asked the land agent. "25,000 yen a *tsubo*," he said. Sixty-nine dollars in U.S. currency.

A tsubo is 3.3 square meters. There were a hundred tsubo, making the total cost $6,900. I could swing it.

The next day we met with the head agent and told him how much we liked the first piece we had seen but that, since it was not on the market, we were very much interested in the one he had shown us.

"Give us a few days to consider," I said.

Three days later, while pacing the low-lying land, we looked up to see three men coming out of the tall grass of the choice lot we wanted above us. Two were in dark suits, neckties, and button-down shirts. The third wore a sweater.

We raced up the hill, breathless.

"Are you fudosanya?" we asked the impeccably dressed two.

"Why yes," they replied as one. "And this is our client."

"Then it is for sale. How much?" I continued.

"Why, 25,000 yen a tsubo."

Our eyes widened.

"We would like to talk to you about it," said Yochan.

The fudosanya said we would have to wait until Monday when their sweatered client would decide if he wanted it. He would call us.

It was Saturday. There was little sleep for us that weekend.

The phone rang Monday morning.

"The client thinks the land is too big. It's 175 tsubo. And he wonders if you would split it with him."

After a whispered consultation, Yochan said we couldn't.

"Then it's yours," the agent said, surely wondering at the eruption of noise at our end.

Lies. Lies. Lies. "Shamisen" Yuchan's people had proven to be as venal as the others. I wanted to phone Yuchan and give him a piece of my mind. Yochan dissuaded me.

"It wouldn't be polite," he said.

Instead, I thanked him for introducing the Kamakura branch office. After all, it had led us to this enchanted hill and to the glorious piece of earth that crowned it, which would soon be ours.

Two days later, we met with the new agent.

"Let me be frank," he said.

We nodded approvingly. Truth was in short supply. We were glad to hear him out.

"It is only fair to tell you," the fudosanya continued, "that though this piece is very fine, indeed, it has one drawback."

We smiled. Whatever it might be, we were prepared to deal with it.

"You see," he said, "like all the others, it has no water."

Had he, like Jove, hurled a thunderbolt at us, the effect could not have been more devastating. Land is like a fish; neither can live long without water.

We looked at each other dumbly. Yochan paled.

It had been a great dream, I thought. Now it was ended. And the minka could go to hell. It wasn't going anywhere.

Other things diverted my attention from the disappointment of the waterless Kamakura land. My old pal Chairman Mao was plotting, with the help of his wife Chiang Ching, a comeback from the oblivion to which the saner members of the Chinese Communist Party had assigned him. His wife had her own agenda: revenge for the past slights of the party moderates. Mao just wanted a second chance to put his crackpot ideas into practice.

Reporting and analyzing these developments kept me busy in the Tokyo office. I also had another distraction: the presidency of the Foreign Correspondents' Club of Japan. I had to be there every day, chair its monthly meetings, and introduce visiting speakers, among them Teddy Kennedy and the Japanese author Yukio Mishima.

We hadn't given up on the land. Not yet, anyway. The agent, a decent fellow, or so we thought, agreed to let me postpone making a down payment until we figured out what to do. We called in a well digger who said he would have to sink a shaft very deep to tap an artesian well and the water, in any case, would be undrinkable. I thought of catchments, like the ones I had seen in Greece. But the Japanese houses have no cellars for storage.

I was still intrigued by the land and thought we ought to make a last effort before giving up on it. So I asked Yochan to send postcards to the other Great Peak landowners in Tokyo, inviting them to the press club to discuss the situation.

About forty-five of them showed up, astonished to see a blond, blue-eyed foreigner presiding over the meeting. Through Yochan I explained the dilemma. One of the owners disclosed that the Minami Company, a developer that once owned the entire hill, had promised to complete the water system years before but gave up after falling on hard times. We decided to see if we could get the company to finish what it had begun.

I did learn one thing as president of the Foreign Correspondents' Club, where I had many dealings with Japanese business types. They never say "no." "*Saa, muzukashii desu*—It's difficult," they would tell you, but it really meant "no."

The Minami people were unfailingly polite. They said they would certainly honor their pledge. They even dug up the old heavy-duty pump they had planned to use when business was better. Alas, years of rust had made it unusable.

One day we got a message from the president of Minami, an unseen presence until then. He offered us some land near Mt. Fuji that we could sell and thus finance the water project. The offer was promising.

A few days later Yochan and I and others of our special committee went to Tokyo to talk with him. It was winter and freezing cold. We sat around the pot-bellied stove and waited. The president showed up two hours late, just as we were getting ready to leave. A tall, white-haired, rumpled figure, his face unusually red, he gave off the aroma of good scotch whiskey.

"I've just concluded a sale," he said. "We had a little celebration."

He emptied his pockets and a shower of 10,000-yen notes fluttered to the floor.

"Whatever you may think, gentlemen," he said, "we certainly aren't short of cash."

He peered intently into my face then, without a word, threw off his jacket, loosened his tie, undid the top two buttons of his trousers, climbed onto a desk, and fell asleep.

The committee chairman, a mild-mannered Tokyo architect, said: "We've had enough. Let's go."

I demurred. "Let's wait until he wakes," I said. "I'd like to ask him about the Fuji land."

We sat around the snoring president, feeling foolish, for another forty minutes until he awakened with a start, rubbing his eyes.

"We have waited for you to awake," I said, "because we want to accept the deeds to the Mt. Fuji land. Thank you for the offer."

The president looked stunned and bewildered.

Yochan interpreted.

"This foreigner does not understand us," he said. "He is from a different culture. As an American he expects a direct answer. A yes or no. It would be rude to say no. The Mt. Fuji land, as you well know, was a goodwill gesture, not to be taken seriously. Please explain that to him."

That was that. The committee bowed itself out, and we gave up on the Minami water option.

A Bad Oyster

The duplicity of the Minami president and what seemed the disappearance of the last, bright hope for bringing water to the Great Peak left me tired, frustrated, and disillusioned. I had begun by hating the idea of owning the Nomura minka, then, bowled over by the bright promise of the Great Peak plot, had begun to think that a home of my own might not be such a wild idea, but I wanted a home more Western than Japanese, one more likely to be livable than the enormous Nomura pile.

I was exhausted by the effort to keep smiling in the face of so much hypocritical deception and began to ask myself whether all the fuss was worth it.

In June 1966, I left this dilemma behind for a while to accept an honorary doctorate from my alma mater, Colby, for my China coverage. I reflected wryly that as a student I knew next to nothing about China or Japan. In fact, my problem then was Chaucer and the language he spoke, which baffled me.

When I returned to Kamakura, Yochan informed me our cherished, waterless piece of land had slipped through our fingers. The agent said he had been offered 30,000 yen a tsubo for it. The disappointment was bitter, but I couldn't blame him. He had waited months for me to make up my mind. I did wonder, however, who would be foolish enough to buy land lacking the most vital ingredient for its use.

Yochan, meanwhile, had been looking around for something else. He showed me a lot in Kita Kamakura. It was too small, too expensive, and didn't have an access road. One would have to be built. I said thanks but no thanks.

The land agents had lied so often to us, I began to doubt this latest story that someone had offered 30,000 yen a tsubo for the plot we so much wanted. It sounded fishy.

I couldn't believe fate had played me such a trick. I was beginning to develop the same sort of passion for this particular parcel of land that the Takishitas had for the minka, and I began to see that I could be as obstinate about something I wanted as they were. It appalled me a bit, but only momentarily.

An unregenerate optimist, I refused to admit defeat. Yochan's father, Katoji, was visiting us. He didn't know the fudosanya we had been dealing with.

"Please call on him," I said, "and find out whether the land is still for sale and whether someone really has offered 30,000 yen a tsubo for it. Don't tell him you know me or Yochan."

Katoji returned from his visit with the fudosanya that night to report that the land hadn't been sold to anyone and that it was still up for sale. And at 25,000 yen a tsubo, the original price!

"Are there no honest people left in Japan?" I cried indignantly. "I thought this man was, but he's been caught in a barefaced lie. Twice, in fact!"

The principled thing to do would have been to break off all contact with this congenital liar. But, water or no water, I wanted my dream quarter-acre so badly it hurt. I wrote out a check for the full amount and asked Katoji to conclude the deal. Yochan supported me.

Katoji telephoned from Tokyo the following night. Yochan paled at what he heard. The office manager announced he had seen the lot, fallen in love with it, bought it, and put it back on the market at 35,000 yen a tsubo!

This was blackmail, pure and simple.

Katoji told us later he had reached down into the richly profane language of his cavalry days to express his reaction to this bit of nasty news.

"And you know what you can do with your lousy old land!" he shouted at the end of a string of words made of flame and molten lava.

I laughed though I really wanted to cry, and told him he had done the right thing, that I would have done the same. I had been a fool to think that I, an ignorant, innocent foreigner, could outwit a fudosanya.

That put the search for land on hold for a few months. Yochan tried to make a joke about it all. Remembering a proverb he had picked up during his English courses at Waseda, he observed: "I guess your friend Shamisen Yuchan led us to the well but we've found there was nothing to drink." I laughed weakly.

Just before Christmas, oysters changed our lives and fortunes. Yochan had a visiting university schoolmate for lunch and decided to serve us raw Hiroshima oysters. Fat and delicious, they are famous all over Asia.

The guest and I ate sparingly, but Yochan wolfed them down. The next day he came down with food poisoning, became delirious, and ran a high fever. Rushed to the nearest hospital—a one-room affair in need of scrubbing—the doctor hooked him up to the usual intravenous drip and went home.

"He'll either be dead or alive tomorrow morning," he said cheerfully. "That's the way it works."

I didn't appreciate the joke. It scared the hell out of me. I felt faint, frightened, and sick to my stomach. It had never occurred to me that our friendship might end with such brutal finality. I felt as though I had fallen off a speeding merry-go-round. It left me dizzy and weak-headed, unable to cope with the thought of existence without him. He would no longer meet me at the door with his quick, youthful smile and affectionate banter. I felt a surge of self-pity, but an even greater sadness for Yochan. It was terribly unfair, I thought, that he should die so young.

Katoji and Kazu hurried down from Shirotori to help me put cold compresses on his burning forehead. I didn't have the courage to tell them what the doctor had predicted.

I cannot remember a night as long and as bleak as this one. I prayed to whatever gods there were that he would pull through. Since the next morning he did, and it was Christmas Day, I assume the Christian one heard me.

Weak and exhausted, Yochan returned to the rented house that afternoon. Katoji had bought a tree and decked it with presents.

Feeling lucky, I decided to push it further.

"The fudosanya told us the other day he sold the Peak land for 35,000 yen a tsubo," I said. "Frankly, after all the lies, I don't believe anything anymore. Kazu, please phone the landowner, not the fudosanya, and find out what's really happening. Tell him you are my secretary."

Yochan got the number, and she phoned Tokyo.

"*Hai, hai, so desu ka,*" she said. "*Domo arigato gozaimasu.*"

"It's still for sale," she said, hand over receiver. "And at 25,000 yen a tsubo. What shall I say?"

Kazu, Katoji, and I cheered. Yochan joined in weakly.

"Tell him it's a sale," I told her.

It was the finest Christmas I have ever celebrated, and I have had many, in many places, including Bethlehem.

The Takishitas, happy that the old minka now could begin its new life on the Great Peak, shared my happiness. I wasn't yet convinced that this was the way I wanted things to turn out, but I didn't say so. It was the wrong moment.

Three days later, my brilliant China-watching colleague George Inagaki, acting as an interpreter, met with the owner and me in a Kamakura coffee shop. Short and pleasant, a man of agreeable manners, the owner accepted the $12,152 in yen that I offered him and bowed. He then returned the equivalent of $3,402.

"Since we concluded the deal directly, without the fudosanya," he said, "I am deducting what would have been their commission."

He said this in such a natural way, as though it was the right thing to do, that my faith in humanity, badly shaken by the fudosanya, suddenly was handsomely restored.

"I wasn't very happy with them anyway," he added.

On the way out, he paused at the door and said, "By the way, you almost didn't get this land. A gentleman from Gifu contacted the fudosanya a few months ago and seemed about to buy it. But for some strange reason, he stormed out in a rage without doing so."

I smiled. Katoji was amused.

Before coming to Japan and meeting the Takishitas, I had never owned anything of value. Now, because of a careless remark made to Yochan at breakfast, I owned a historic fourteen-dollar minka and one of the most exciting pieces of land I had seen anywhere, in all my travels.

Two days later, Yochan phoned the Tokyo landlords. Since the Minami negotiations had fallen through, he said, would any of them be interested in chipping in enough money to complete the water system? Twenty said they would. It would take $200 each.

Two weeks later we met at the Zeniarai Benten Shrine halfway up the hill and formed the "Omine Kai," the Great Peak Water Association, with me as temporary chairman.

So now the land was mine and in a few months it, and that of the other owners, would at last receive the water that would make all our property viable. It had been a long, wearing, discouraging fight, concluded in the final moments with bewildering speed. In retrospect it all looked so easy, I wondered why it had been so complicated.

The Takishitas interpreted the victory as a mandate for arousing the disembodied minka from its slumber and resurrecting it on the Great Peak. I continued to hope, wanly and secretly, that they would forget about it and I could raise enough money to put up a cheap, imported-cedar house complete with fireplace, bay windows, and central heating. I saw myself sitting on the terrace smoking my pipe and thoughtfully sipping a dry martini. I knew I was whistling in the dark. The Takishitas, I had by now learned, were an elemental force of nature against which I could not presume to prevail.

I stroll the uninhabited, waterless Great Peak with Yochan's brother Katsumi, Kazu and Katoji in the rear.

Tin!

During the winter of 1966–67, Yochan neglected his Waseda
studies to pore over a coffee table book in Japanese on minkas.
Published by Bijutsu Shuppan-sha in 1962, it was the definitive
technical work on Japanese folk houses. John Weatherhill
brought out an English translation that winter under the title
The Essential Japanese House. The variety and external beauty
of the minkas shown in these books aroused my grudging
admiration. I particularly liked their thatch roofs. Molded to the
buildings in imaginative ways—some looked like caps, others
had pointed eaves, like horse ears—they evoked memories of the
human past; early man lived in just such houses in nearly every
country.

But the photographs, no matter how compelling, did not
deceive me. I knew from experience that their interiors—cold,
dark, and dank—were fit more for animals than humans. I knew
the Takishitas were determined to transplant the Nomura minka
to the Great Peak. But I wondered, almost in despair, if they really
expected me to live in it.

In the ensuing winter months, Kazu, Katoji, Yochan, and
I were invited to the home of my friend Meredith Weatherby, the
Weatherhill publisher. His interest in folk houses dated back ten
years earlier to when he had acquired one, taken it down, and
rebuilt it in the bustling Tokyo entertainment district of Roppongi.

Tall, easy-going, an artist in his own right, Meredith had
unerring good taste. He spoke Japanese fluently, had been a career
foreign-service officer, gone into publishing, and translated two of

Yukio Mishima's books, *Confessions of a Mask* and *The Sound of Waves.*

He warned us that minkas were hard to heat. Sitting in front of his handsome but ineffectual Swedish porcelain stove, we could not but agree. Niggardly about his own comfort, he could have solved the problem with central heating. I wondered why he hadn't.

Meredith's architect took a rather plain minka and re-created it to his own taste. The result was striking. Meredith enlivened the interior with old scrolls and the works of modern Japanese sculptors whom he encouraged. A classical Japanese garden outside completed the illusion of perfection.

Though I hoped nothing would come of it, I found in myself a growing interest in architecture, particularly of the Japanese kind. The old Imperial Hotel, which I often visited, was one of Frank Lloyd Wright's great creations. Reading his autobiography, I was intrigued by this paragraph: "I knew well that no house should ever be *on* a hill or *on* anything. It should be *of* the hill. Belonging to it. Hill and house should live together each the happier for the other."

I got the point. But Wright, ever the artist, offered no clues on how I might make livable this house married to its hill.

There is a moment in the building of a house when the owners make the quantum leap from vision to reality. Stakes are driven in the still, hard earth and strings attached to them to outline how it will look on the ground. It is a simple but deeply moving experience. Here, after all the estimates and planning, the hopes and despair, one takes the first concrete steps in the building process. Fancy begins to approach reality. For Yochan it meant imminent fulfillment of the promise he had made two years before to find me a house of my own. It marked the end of my resistance to that promise and acceptance of the Nomura minka, warts and all, as my future home. Walking through the outlined rooms, I wanted to cry out for joy as I gazed out over the woods, the bay, and the city of Kamakura below and reflected that whatever happened, whether the minka proved livable or not, I had this glorious vista to console me.

When I bought it, the land looked huge, but now I was astonished to find the Nomura minka much bigger that I thought. Once it had been re-erected, there wouldn't be much land left over: a chunk in front and modest spaces on either side. Never mind, I thought, we've come this far. Not to worry.

Now that this first step had been taken, the serious thinking about what kind of house I wanted began. Like most prospective house builders I did not lack for advice. Friends suggested cannibalizing the minka for its spectacular beams and installing them in a modern, easily heated building. Yochan, magnanimous in victory and concerned over the sorry state of my finances, said it would be cheaper to sacrifice the immense snow roof and jettison the second floor, leaving a still-large one-story house with a flat roof. I was touched, realized how painful it was for Yochan to even think of such a possibility, and flatly vetoed it.

"If we're going to do it, let's do it right," I said. "A minka isn't a minka unless it has that magnificent steep roof."

Tanaka, the city councilman who had overseen the dismantling of the Nomura minka and had been asked to put it up again on the Great Peak, arrived in Kamakura for consultations. Short, near-sighted, and fussy, he did not inspire confidence.

Over green tea and sweet cakes, I told him I hoped the minka in its reincarnation would reflect the Japanese ideal of *shibui*: restrained, simple, but elegant. I was talking through my hat, hadn't the faintest idea what shibui really meant. But then neither did Tanaka.

The beautiful roofs of the coffee table–book minkas and their impressive wood and plaster walls appeared in my mind as I talked.

"What," I genially asked Tanaka after a sip of tea, "did you use for the roofs of those forty minkas you took down, moved, and rebuilt?"

"Why, tin!" he replied as though he had never heard the word shibui.

I paled.

"Not thatch?"

"Oh dear no. That takes time. At least three years to gather. And money. Lots of money. People around here don't have that much time and certainly not that much money."

"And the walls?"

"Tin, of course. Same's the roof. It's what everyone wants."

On the way out Tanaka asked me how much I had budgeted for rebuilding the Nomura minka. Incautiously—Yochan had not yet warned me—I said 3,600,000 yen, the equivalent of $10,000.

Yochan and Katoji, far from shocked by Tanaka's love of tin, supported him.

Houses with tin roofs are everywhere in the countryside," said Yochan. "They're cheap, easy to install and maintain. I know you love thatch and so do I. It's beautiful. There's nothing like it. But John-san, let's be practical. You really can't afford thatch even if you could wait a couple of years to find it."

The disappointment showed in my face.

"Look, John-san, tin can look good too. If it's properly designed it can be quite handsome."

"I understand what you're saying, Yochan. And thank you for worrying about the cost. It's only that I'd like the minka to look like the original. It had thatch. And it looked great. It wasn't tin."

Yochan smiled.

"Believe me, if they could have had it, the Nomuras also would have used tin."

"Then what about the walls? You want tin walls on our house?"

"No. I agree with you there. They should be of wood and plaster."

It was my first encounter with the realities of rural Japan. It was true, there were quite a few old minkas with thatch roofs in the countryside, but there were more with tin ones. I just hadn't noticed.

The Shirotori farmers loved thatch. It reminded them of a not-too-distant past when the entire village turned out to help install it on newly built minkas. They regretted the passing of the team spirit and community mindedness of that era. The generation that might have been expected to continue these traditions, Yochan's generation, the postwar one, had abandoned the villages for Tokyo and Osaka, where the big corporations invoked village virtues to achieve their enormous profits.

Farmers represented nearly 30 percent of the population at war's end, but with industrialization in the 1960s, this had shrunk to 6 percent. Though fewer in number, they remained conservative, like Katoji and Kazu.

They would have preferred thatch for my roof but they, too, recognized the utility of tin.

"It can be molded into all kinds of shapes. And it's fireproof," Katoji said.

I said I'd think about it. But I really wanted thatch.

The project got rolling in March, immediately after Yochan's graduation from Waseda with the law degree he never got to use. I had reason to be grateful for Yochan's bulldog tenacity. Now I discovered this easygoing youth also had an almost terrifying capacity for concentration. He shut out everything—me, Waseda, the world—as he zeroed in on "A Minka for John-san," the words etched in his concentrated, absorbed, totally focused mind.

Two days after graduation he went to Shirotori to organize the disassembled minka's move to Kamakura.

While there he checked out the condition of the timbers and consulted with Tanaka. They discussed the move to Kamakura and sat down to work out the cost. Then the roof, figuratively speaking, fell in. Tanaka presented his estimates. They totaled the equivalent of $9,500.

"That didn't include the roof, the walls, the plumbing, or the electricity," Yochan told me in a strangled voice over the phone. "Only the skeleton. I begged him to lower the figure. He refused. Why did you have to tell him how much you had? I don't know what we can do. I'm afraid it's all over."

He paused then broke into sobs. "I'm sorry, John-san. Please forgive me. I've let you down. This is the blackest day of my life."

The realization of how much Yochan, usually taciturn, had invested emotionally and physically in finding me a home stunned me even more than the news of Tanaka's perfidy. It moved me so deeply I was unable for almost a minute to say anything.

"Hello, hello, are you there?" asked Yochan.

"Yes, yes. Please forgive me. My mind was wandering. I just want to tell you how grateful I am for everything you and your family have done to get us this far. And now I'm going to sound like you and say that we mustn't give up. Nothing is impossible. I know because my haragei, my gut instinct, tells me so."

Yochan laughed faintly. But he seemed a little relieved.

"I'll dig around and see what can be done," he said. "It doesn't look good. I'll let you know."

Four days later an exuberant Yochan phoned Kamakura.

"John-san! John-san!" he cried. "Good news. Katoji refused to surrender. He beat the bushes and discovered a team of young carpenters willing to do the job. They'll charge a flat fee, well within your budget."

"Wonderful. Congratulations. I knew the Takishitas would refuse to say die. Now my question is, do these young carpenters know anything about reassembling a minka? I gather it's rather a special skill."

"Glad you asked," said Yochan cheerfully. "The answer is no. N-O. But they've seen them, of course. And the minka's features are almost the same as the modern houses they've been working on. Anyway, they say they are quick learners, and they are eager to try."

The next day the new team broke open the shed and with the help of Yochan, Katoji, and assorted Takishita cousins loaded the disembodied timbers of the Nomura minka into ten huge trucks. It was a full day's work. They went to bed early that night and were up at midnight to begin the thirteen-hour journey to Kamakura.

Sitting in the lead truck Yochan, exhausted, gave the signal to roll and the strange caravan, loaded with the massive relics of another age, slowly lumbered out of Shirotori in a driving rainstorm. It was a historic occasion of sorts. No mountain minka from Gifu had ever gone so far. The irony was that this particular minka had only recently been owned by the descendants of the Heike, the ill-fated military clan whose brief days of glory were ended by the Kamakura shogun eight hundred years before.

The convoy reached the outskirts of Kamakura at one o'clock in the afternoon of the same day and met resistance from the police. They had not been forewarned of the appearance of this Heike host. Theirs was a more mundane consideration: they feared the trucks would snarl Kamakura traffic. Directed to a vacant lot north of the Great Peak, the trucks parked there until nightfall. Yochan, Katoji, and Kazu sped in a taxi to my rented house where, elated, they announced the convoy's safe arrival.

But the difficulties in this capital of the twelfth-century victor continued. At sunset the first truck moved up the narrow road leading to the Great Peak and was unable because of its length to negotiate the hairpin curve that led to the building site.

Awakened from a fitful nap, Yochan telephoned a friend in nearby Hayama who loaned him his half-ton truck. This was a break, but the operation had to wait until the following day. Once it began, progress was slow and discouraging. The pillars and beams had to be unloaded and brought, one at a time, to the site. Instead of one trip by ten trucks, it took fifty by one small one to deliver the precious cargo. Friendship in Japan means something; the owner of the half-ton truck indignantly refused to be paid.

Once the lone truck had deposited a small mountain of building materials on the wide path on the east of my property there could be no doubt that the Nomura minka was about to rise again in the capital of the Heike's old enemy.

(top) A forty-five-foot beam, the first of many, rides on a two-ton truck to the site, Yochan at the wheel.

(bottom) Sturdy carpenters carry it on their shoulders to the work area.

In Japan nothing goes unnoticed. The flurry of activity came to the attention in some still-mysterious way of the owner sharing the other half of the common pathway. He had not attended the Tokyo meeting and showed no interest in the subsequent group effort to bring water to the Great Peak. But now out of the blue, he sent a message to me: "Move the building materials off my half of the path. At once." It was not an auspicious beginning. The carpenters laboriously did so. Our neighbor's unfriendly action foreshadowed a dispute over the right of way. But that was in the future.

Workers cut the grass and a small bulldozer leveled the building site, after which the carpenters announced they were ready to go. They planned to finish the job in twenty-five days. Told this, I whistled in disbelief.

Two things had to be done before the carpenters could get to work. They participated in the first, a solemn appeasement of the earth god, and went sightseeing in Kamakura during the second, the laying of the minka's foundation.

The Tsurugaoka Hachiman Shrine, built in the year 1063 by an ancestor of Japan's first shogun, Yoritomo, supplied the Shinto priest who presided over the earth ceremonies. I wondered whether anyone in the shrine, dedicated to the god of war, knew or cared that a Heike minka was about to rise on one of the highest hills of the ancient capital.

If the Hachiman priest had any misgivings, he did not show them. Young, bespectacled, and voluble, he came to the Great Peak in Yochan's car, bringing with him a small portable altar and offerings of fruit, vegetables, fish, and sake to the hungry and thirsty gods.

Before beginning the proceedings, called *jichinsai*, he slipped into his ceremonial robes—a silk jacket, sharply pressed gray pantaloons, and a tall black lacquered hat. I thought of Nomura and his tattered silk jacket and reflected that men may change, but religion and its rites do not.

Chanting ancient prayers, prayers as old as Japanese civilization, the priest invoked the earth gods then apologized for disturbing their habitat. He scattered squares of white paper, denoting purity, north, south, east, and west, then waved a branch of the sacred sakaki tree over the earth, the altar, and the assembled company. In the final act, I, as the owner, led Yochan, Kazu, Katoji, the carpenters, and Uncle Nakaichi (Kazu's brother) in laying branches of the same sakaki tree on the altar. I held mine in both hands, bowed, approached the altar, bowed again, gently deposited the branch, faced the priest, and bowed once more.

For me, a Roman Catholic *non pratiquant*, as the French would say—more plainly a "back slider" to my more devout brothers—the ceremony had a freshness and natural quality missing from the mass. This was hardly surprising. Shinto, the most ancient of Japanese religions, worships nature. The Takishitas also were comfortable with it as well as Buddhism, whose incense burning, candles, and chants resemble Catholicism. Asked to choose, I think I would opt for Shinto and its millions of gods. Something for everyone.

Uncle Nakaichi took over where the priest had left off. He directed laying of the foundation, a desecration of the consecrated earth for which the Shinto priest had sought forgiveness from the gods. But before he could do his job, Uncle Nakaichi needed water. There wouldn't be any for another three months.

"What am I to do?" he asked me. "In my business one needs sand and cement, but above all, water."

Yochan grinned. "Don't worry, Uncle," he said. "You shall have it."

He jumped into the old van I had bought for the construction project and raced to the nearby public park where he "borrowed" water from its public water fountains. He filled dozens of two-gallon cans, hurried back, and poured the purloined water into a large drum can, one of two at the site. It was hard, punishing work. The sharp metal handles of the cans bit into his hands, drawing blood. As long as I had known him, with the exception of the oyster poisoning, Yochan had never complained of pain or discomfort. He didn't this time, either.

The water supplied tea, a necessity, for the carpenters, besides making the mixing of the concrete possible. Astonished at their capacity for gulping down vast quantities of green tea, I was hard put to say which was more vital to the project, cement or tea.

Kamakura is earthquake territory. It was destroyed by the Great Kanto Quake of 1923, which leveled Tokyo and claimed 123,000 lives. The Great Peak is lashed at certain times of the year by typhoon or near-typhoon winds. Uncle Nakaichi considered these facts and decided against positioning the minka posts on round stones as they had been in Ise. He poured instead a Western-style foundation, the posts held in place by steel clamps attached to it. There was some talk about hooking steel cables to the roof to keep it from flying off on the next high wind. But Yochan and I vetoed this idea. We felt reasonably sure the clamps would do the job.

Honorable Daiku-san

In my eight years in Japan, up to the building of the minka, I had come to know two specialized classes: journalists and land agents, fudosanya. The journalists, *shinbun kisha*, are my kind of people; well-educated, intelligent, driven by the same passion to know what makes people tick that had persuaded me to choose reporting as a career. I counted many of them as friends. The fudosanya were another kettle of fish; after months of unpleasant encounters with a dozen of them I had a low opinion of real estate agents in general.

In 1967 I encountered yet another group: carpenters, or *daiku*. Like the *fudosanya-san* they were usually referred to by the honorific *san*: as in *daiku-san*, or honorable carpenters. Though I did not yet know them well enough to pass judgment, what I had heard from the Takishitas predisposed me to like and trust them. They were well qualified to speak. The mountain area of Gifu where they lived had been the home of master carpenters for centuries, the most skilled in all Japan. So great was their expertise they were the preferred choice of emperors, abbots, princes, and court ladies in the highly sophisticated Heian Era from 794 to 1185 AD. They were, in fact, literally too brilliant for their own good. They were so valuable the emperor didn't want them to leave, not even to visit their homes and families. Like birds in a gilded cage, he heaped on them wealth, honors, and imperial favor, but denied them the one thing they most cherished: freedom.

Like their forebears, the carpenters who came to Kamakura from Shirotori had spent years under a master carpenter who clothed and fed them and acted as their surrogate father and role model. They began training at eleven and stayed under his tutelage for five or six years. Totally cut off from their families, they gave him their unquestioning obedience and loyalty. In exchange he revealed to them the mysteries of his art. The course was hard and demanding, the living conditions spartan. They were being initiated not only to a profession but an almost holy brotherhood. Before they could pick up the sacred tools that were to sustain their lives, the master carpenter had to be convinced they had achieved the required spiritual and professional level.

The master carpenter for the Great Peak project was a sturdy, round-faced, thirty-three-year-old friend of Yochan's named Taichi Miwa. After a week on the job, Yochan and I agreed he probably could be trusted to do anything in construction. He gave off such an air of quiet self-confidence I went a step further and decided he was the man I would want to captain my lifeboat.

He had spent six years as an apprentice under a tough master and had another twelve years of experience before coming to this job. Married with two children, his passion was fishing, a fact I found oddly reassuring. Anglers have monumental patience. And they don't panic. I could boast of neither of these qualities.

He had heard good things about me from Yochan and the rest of the Takishita clan, but he had never met an American and had his reservations about them.

"They build houses and cover them with paint," he grumbled to Katoji.

Americans, it is hardly necessary to observe, paint their houses to make them attractive and waterproof. Reflecting their love of nature and the natural, the Japanese build their houses in unpainted wood. They admire its grain, its knots and whorls, and

The first act in man's ageless drama—building a home—has begun.
I sit stunned beside the central pillar.

its colors. They love to see it age with the changing weather so that the house it covers looks, as Frank Lloyd Wright put it, *of* the hill rather than *on* it.

"Don't worry Miwakun," said Katoji, using the familiar form to address the master carpenter. "John-san hasn't the faintest idea of putting paint on this house. Not a speck. He's American, I grant you. But he understands that this is an old minka, and you don't put paint on an old minka."

Miwa grudgingly accepted this explanation but kept a wary eye out for any sign of paint, brush, or paint can.

Of the other carpenters two stood out. Yasuo Bito, also thirty-three, short, red-faced, shy, was a true individual. His credentials were unusual. He was one of half a dozen Japanese carpenters who a few years earlier had taken a city minka to New York and set it up in the courtyard of the Museum of Modern Art. Everyone involved in that project had been a specialist but responded to the whip of the master carpenter.

Bito produced a well-thumbed magazine article with photos of himself and the minka. A deliberate, sweet-tempered man, he was primarily an artist. He insisted on going at his own pace as work proceeded, something no master carpenter would accept. But Bito was so famous in the countryside that no one objected. His independence and skills made him almost unemployable in Gifu, where solidity and predictability in construction tend to be valued over the unusual.

Sculpture was his true calling. He made a Statue of Liberty, a remarkable likeness, for Yochan's cousin's restaurant after the old biplane that had been there went out of fashion. Several years after working on my minka, he opened a school to teach the rough, many-planed wood sculpture made famous by the great Enku, an eighteenth-century native of the Gifu mountains.

By common consent Yochan was the project's field marshal, advising and consulting me, plotting the overall strategy, and arranging for the various performers to come in on cue. Miwa was the project's commanding general on the scene, making the day-to-day decisions. Nobu Sumi, sturdy, square-shouldered, intelligent, was, to continue the martial metaphor, its chief of staff, responsible for recruiting the workers, keeping them supplied,

Daiku-san Kaneshige Etori smooths a beam with a plane.

and acting as inspector general. A master carpenter in his own right, he commanded respect both because he was older and, more importantly, paymaster. He too had initial doubts about me.

"He's an American," he said to Katoji, "a rich American, I suppose. So why does he choose to live in a drafty old minka, the kind we throw away, rather than have us build him a solid, handsome new house, something both of us could be proud of?"

Katoji grinned.

"You may not believe this," he said, "but there are *gaijin* who love these old minkas. Why, I visited one in Tokyo that had been redone and was very grand. John-san likes the style and the size."

I learned of this conversation somewhat later. Had I been able to reply, I might have told Sumi I agreed with him wholeheartedly. I had seen how well Japanese carpenters built modern houses, and even without paint I would have given my eyeteeth to have one. But that was water—or should I say paint—over the dam. Sumi didn't know about my own original hesitations, and at this late date when the die had been cast, I wasn't about to tell him.

The other carpenters—there were six in all—were pleasant, hard-working types. They had considerable fun at the expense of the youngest, Sadao Kuriki, twenty-four, fresh-faced, earnest, a very recent bridegroom.

"Shouldn't you be home making babies?" they asked him. Wives didn't accompany daiku-san on their out-of-town jobs.

Blushing deeply, he refused to see the humor of it all. Just graduated from his apprenticeship, he prided himself on his skills, desperately wanted to be accepted for himself. Because of this he worked more and played less than the others. In a few weeks he became one of them.

It is hard to describe the provincialism of these Gifu carpenters. Their world centered around the small cities and villages of the Gifu mountains and the prefectural capital, Gifu City. Few had in their lifetime visited Tokyo, even fewer Kamakura. For them this was an adventure to be savored as well as a job to be done. In later years, thanks to Yochan, they would make journeys they had never dreamt possible. But in 1967 they were an eager,

Daiku-san Taizou Miwa works in what is to become the living room.

unspoiled, innocent lot, courteous, well-behaved, but amused
and intrigued by foreigners and foreign ways.

They may not have been worldly wise but they were very
much aware of their own worth. First-class professionals, they had
been taught during their apprenticeships to regard their calling
as something akin to sacred and to take exceptional pride in what
they did. The gods of Shinto surrounded them, and they paid them
homage. There was a working relationship between them and the
eternal spirits of nature, from whom they drew their inspiration
and their strength. The very tools with which they worked were
considered sacred.

Because the minka's primary beams and pillars are held
together not by nails, but by wooden pegs and joinery, large
wooden mallets were used to knock them apart and pound them

together again. I have vivid memories of the daiku-san silhouetted against the lowering sky as they wielded their heavy mallets during the dismantling in Ise. Nothing had changed over the centuries. The Nomura ancestors employed the same kind of tool to put the old house together in 1734.

Some of the enormous beams in the Nomura house, and indeed all *gassho* farmhouses in the snow country, were curved. Called *chona bari*, they achieved their curvature naturally. Planted on steep hillsides, pressed down by the heavy weight of the snow—ten feet deep in severe winters—the young saplings grow out and upward, searching for the sun. Japanese farmers are patient. They wait years for them to grow into full size. Installed in the gassho they act as an arch, supporting the heavy weight of the snow-laden roof and opening up more space in the large interior.

The curvature also satisfied a philosophical Japanese love for the irregular and unusual. Many Japanese works of art, particularly clay pots, slightly flawed at the collar, remind us that life is imperfect. The curved beams and their gardens are also a reflection of this Zen philosophy.

As though to prove that they can do it, the Japanese carpenter from the oldest time has created beams both perfectly straight and smooth. They do so with a primitive adze, called a *chona*, ancestor of the modern plane, which they also use today.

Dating from the thirteenth century, the chona is a wedge of very sharp steel at the end of a curved wooden handle. It is pulled, like Japanese saws, chisels, and planes, toward the body rather than away from it, as are Western tools.

I winced more than once as I watched the daiku-san vigorously wielding this instrument. Missing toes and wounds on the feet and legs attest to its lethal qualities. In the right hands

Yochan, his aunt Kakehi, and Kazu below the most massive transverse curved beam

it makes beams remarkably smooth, as though they had been machine tooled.

Perhaps the most beautiful of the ancient tools is the *sumitsubo,* used to draw a straight line on wood prior to sawing or splitting it. Modern carpenters perform this chore a thousand times a day with a simple straightedge, but many Japanese carpenters insist on the sumitsubo. I am convinced they do so because it is difficult, they like to be different, and the instrument itself is a work of art. Yochan conceded these points but insisted the sumitsubo had practical advantages over the modern way: it draws a straighter and longer line.

Not easy to describe, it looks like a wooden Dutch shoe with an inkpad in the sole and a spool wound with a thin line high up in the heel. When it is drawn out, the line runs over the inkpad, emerging as black as coal. Pulled out to the desired length on the piece of wood it is to mark, it is then pinned to the spot with a thumbtack. What happens then is more like music than carpentry. The daiku-san plucks the taut string as a cellist would to create a pizzicato and in so doing leaves a perfectly straight black line on the wood.

Carpenters lavish their love on the sumitsubo. They make them in wondrous shapes, decorate them with metal or mother-of-pearl, coat them in lacquer, or inscribe them with their signatures. I have a few; Meredith Weatherby's collection is outstanding.

Though they used an astonishing number of old tools, the Gifu carpenters brought with them many modern ones, as well. The buzzing of hacksaws, ripsaws, and god only knows how many other saws—hand-held and electric—mingled with the sound of mallets, metal hammers striking iron nails, and the high whine of power tools, sounded to me like a symphony orchestra warming up. I couldn't get enough of it.

On the third day after the foundation had set, Yochan announced a great drama was about to take place: the raising of the *daikoku bashira*, the central pillar of the minka. Shinto has it that this giant post holding up an umbrella of beams tied to the primary structure is nothing less than a deity, one of the eight million gods enshrined in its pantheon. The area immediately around it is sacred and must be approached with care and reverence.

Everyone but a handful of workers downed tools to watch this event. Long and heavy, it had to be handled with skill and brawn to avoid its crashing to the ground, an ill omen to be avoided at all costs. Ropes were attached to its top and, in a technique as old as the hills, one set of carpenters pulled it into a shaky upright position while, opposite, another set steadied it. Once up, boards were nailed to its midsection to hold it in place as its attendant beams—seven in the Nomura minka—were fitted in place like tree branches. These were joined to more pillars fixed at intervals into the foundation. Within an hour a recognizable structure emerged where none had existed before.

This first visible sign of reconstruction touched off a celebration. Yochan produced large bottles of sake and plates of peanuts, dried squid, and salted soybeans. The toasts were numerous and heartfelt. The Takishitas beamed on me and I returned their smiles with unfeigned pleasure. Building a house, or just buying one, must be one of man's highest pleasures, along with love, sex, food, and drink. Once so indifferent, even hostile to the idea, I had begun to share the Takishitas' enthusiasm. Raising the daikoku bashira created an inner excitement I had never before experienced, and I decided it came partly from the pleasurable feeling one gets from owning a house, instead of merely renting it. I reflected that I was on the verge of becoming, in a small way, a member of the bourgeoisie. What would Mao have thought?

Once the daikoku bashira assumed its rightful place at the center of the reborn minka, assembling the first-floor primary structure, the load-bearing part of the building, moved briskly ahead. The posts and beams were held together by the tongue-and-groove method. "Tongues" deftly shaped at the ends of the beams slid into grooves cut into the top part of each post. Small wooden pegs hammered into the protruding tongues kept the whole assembly from flying apart in a heavy earthquake or a high wind. This interlocking system is loose and flexible, absorbing shocks like a cat's cradle.

Katoji explained that tongue-and-groove is widely used where minkas are subjected to unusual stresses and strains. Elsewhere the heavy beams are simply placed on top of the posts and kept in place by their weight, much in the same way the ancient Greeks built their marble temples. To me this seemed more dangerous than tongue-and-groove. Thinking back on Japanese earthquakes and the ruins I had seen in Athens, I wholeheartedly approved of this method, also known as mortise and tenon.

Though the primary and secondary structures were innocent of nails, plans called for the use of hundreds of them in the floors, ceilings, walls, and other additions to these central building blocks.

As the construction proceeded I was astonished to see how many beams supported the floor: twenty of them, each about six inches in diameter. I thought so many floor underpinnings unnecessary considering the not intolerable weight they would handle. Yochan pointed out they were an integral part of the skeletal framework, giving it a solid, non-rigid bottom to counteract the heavy roof and the inevitable pulls and pushes it would undergo in a major quake or typhoon. One thing was undeniable: when the Nomuras built in 1734, they built to last.

Using only a block and tackle—I could not afford even the smallest mechanical crane—the carpenters completed the

Etori Kaneshige preparing to create a window sill on one of the pillars.

basic first floor, sans walls, ceilings, or floorboards, in ten days. The speed at which these small, self-effacing, polite carpenters moved astonished me. It was hard, sweaty, backbreaking work, but they didn't pause except for an occasional tea break. They were racing against the clock; Miwa predicted the minka would be completed within twenty-five days. The sooner it was finished, the sooner everyone could go home.

Taking time off from the office, I managed to spend several hours a day at the site. Never an early riser—I subscribe to Oscar Wilde's determination to do anything to succeed except get up early and do exercises—I arrived hours after Yochan and the workers, who were there from dawn to 10 PM. For a while I was puzzled: something was missing. There were no blueprints. I had seen dozens of them in visits to Maine construction sites in my youth. Miwa worked instead from a thin board called an *itazu*, which had been used to put up the

Nomura minka in 1734. This antique blueprint of sorts had lain hidden, like the fire-and-ice poem found in the tokonoma, for more than two centuries. Katoji found it nailed to the underside of a floorboard.

The itazu indicated in ink the location of the various posts, doors, and windows. Since the height of minka posts is very nearly standard all over Japan, there was no need to mark in the elevations.

Another detail made Miwa's job easier. Walls in some Western buildings hold up the floors above and the roof. In Japanese minkas the posts serve this function. This makes it easy to move the walls around at will, even eliminate them entirely. This is the "hanging wall" principle. Adopted many years later in the West, it makes skyscrapers possible. In minkas and even modern Japanese homes, interior rooms shrink and expand according to need without compromising the integrity of the structure.

The upside-down U-shape of the first floor beams and pillars seen against the setting sun reminded me of a wooden version on a smaller scale of Stonehenge in England. I had seen this ancient stone monument to the gods once while I lived in London. The unfinished minka embodied, in my romantic eyes, the same mysterious worship of nature that inspired the early Britons.

With the first-floor skeleton intact, the daiku-san now embarked on their most difficult and dangerous phase: tackling the second floor and raising the massive roof.

Miwa works on the polished floor of the North Room areas.

Spider Men

Enter the *tobi*. Dressed in flared trousers, emblazoned *happi* coats, tight leggings, and *hachimaki,* like towels wrapped around their heads, they are among the oldest, most respected, and most skilled of Japanese construction workers. It is easier to say what they do than to translate the word into English. They are the spider men who cover a construction site, no matter how tall—some work on skyscrapers—in canvas lashed to scaffoldings of wood, bamboo, or iron pipe. They and the carpenters and other workers concealed behind this curtain go about their chores, using the scaffolds to move around. One day, the job done, the scaffolding is whipped away with a magician's flare and hey, presto! the completed building is revealed to the astonished gaze.

The tobi excel at great heights, scampering sure-footed among the beams and pillars like agile monkeys. I had seen them perform atop tall ladders during the New Year celebrations at the Tsurugaoka Hachiman Shrine in Kamakura. Like the crowds looking on, I gasped as, at the end of intricate acrobatics, they fell, only to be caught short by long belts attached to the top of the ladders.

Ropes and the block and tackle had been sufficient to put up the first-floor pillars and beams. Raising the heavy roof beams with a crane, though it has its peril, would not have been difficult, but using only rope and tackle, it is downright dangerous and unpredictable. The carpenters could not do it alone. They needed the tobi.

There were eight pairs of roof beams in the Nomura minka, each one forming an approximately equilateral open-based triangle. The trick was to raise them, hold them in place, and then attach them to a long but insubstantial ridgepole running the minka's length from east to west.

When the daiku-san began their hazardous performance the beams were detached and leaning against the west end of the structure waiting to become structural. Working together, using the primitive tools at their disposal, the daiku and tobi lifted them to the second floor and positioned them for the complex and demanding next move.

Each of these beams weighed hundreds of pounds. Their bases were sharpened like pencils to fit into holes in the floor beams while their tops were notched in tongue-and-groove fashion to lock together with each other at the top. The daiku laid them flat and arranged them in the triangles they had once been and now were to become again.

They then nailed a length of thin board across the middle of the first triangle, creating a huge letter A. This kept the slanted beams rigid and in place while ropes were wrapped around each triangle's apex. Inserting the triangle's legs in the floor holes created to receive them, they paused to consider the next step, one that would demand the greatest skill and timing. Using long ropes tied to the apex, they slowly and with infinite care pulled the A to a vertical position. It then was held momentarily in place by thin boards nailed to the floor beams. A single misstep would have been calamitous.

This process was repeated until all eight were lashed with straw rope to the flimsy ridgepole. I watched all this wondering whether so shaky an assembly, not securely anchored, might

Using mallets, just as the carpenters of Ise did in 1734, the daiku-san ceremoniously install the roof ridge pole; uncle Kakehi, Yochan, and Katoji watch below.

collapse in the next quake or typhoon. Before I had time to ask, the daiku propped six more beams against the east and west triangles at either end of the roof. Like flying buttresses in a cathedral, they immensely strengthened the entire roof system. Now reassured, I sat back with a sigh of relief.

Raising the roof beams took two entire days. I watched nervously with Yochan as the process slowly unfolded. During that time the workers flirted more than once with disaster. The tobi, quick and agile, raced to every danger point to save the day. Without them the roof structure might have crashed thirty feet to the ground, endangering not only the entire project but also the lives of those involved.

The roof beams meeting as they did at the top resembled fingers joined in prayer. The Japanese have given this effect a name, and an architectural style: *gassho zukuri*. I began to believe that this minka indeed was touched by divine grace. As if he read my feelings, Yochan called a halt and summoned the Hachiman priest to preside over yet another ceremony, this one celebrating raising the roof, or *muneage shiki*.

The most important of the Shinto building rites, it marked the essential completion of the minka even though much remained to be done. As in the ground-breaking ceremonies, there were offerings of food, purification of the building, and the solemn offering of branches of the sakaki.

The carpenters and I wrote our names on a thin piece of board while the abbot invoked the gods on the other side. Climbing up the beams with the ease of a gymnast, one of the tobi affixed the board to the highest point of the eastern triangle.

Pausing while munching on the delicacies Yochan had provided for the occasion, I wondered what someone might think

A Shinto priest purifies the ground in front of the daikoku bashira before mollifying the gods with offerings of fruit, sake, and dried squid.

two hundred years later when he or she came across this roof board with its single American name among the many Japanese ones.

Though the roof beams were in place, the roof was not. The carpenters, eager to get a covering over their heads so they could work in sunshine and rain, pressed Yochan to decide what kind of roof he wanted. He could have told them it was tin, but since he knew how I felt about that, he asked me instead.

"After what Tanaka told me about thatch and how difficult it is to get, I'm not so enthusiastic about it," I said. Yochan brightened. "But I like it so much I'd like to see whether it's possible. Would you mind calling the fire department and ask if it would approve?"

Dressed to the nines, I brush my name on a munafuda board to be placed with those of the carpenters at the very top of the ancient, unwanted, resurrected minka.

(top) Carpenters begin laying the wooden sheath that will support the roof.
(bottom) Yochan and I raise a glass to toast progress so far.

(top) Heavy ropes and slats the color of thatch hold the beams together and lay a base for the roof covering.

(bottom) A gossamer thing of old wooden beauty

Old friend Reuters correspondent David Chipp shoots the breeze with me as the minka takes shape.

Yochan knew it was a wild-goose chase but called anyway.

"The fire chief says thatch is inflammable and has been banned in Japan for at least a century," he reported the next day. "If you have a house with the original thatch on it, you can replace parts of it when it becomes thin or worn. But in your case, since this will in effect be a new building, it cannot have a thatch roof."

"Why do you have to ask them?" Yochan asked. "Why not use tin? It's cheap and not bad looking."

I put my fingers in my ears.

"Much as I love you, and all your family," I replied, "I will not have tin. I'm sorry but I've made up my mind."

While I dithered, Uncle Nakaichi came up with an idea.

"Thirty years ago," he said, "I roofed a house in cedar shingles. It was cheap and beautiful. Shall I see if the dealer is alive and still in business?"

I told him to order enough to cover the roof. The Takishitas and the daiku-san, impatiently waiting for me to make a decision, cheered.

The next day, I got cold feet. Cedar is wood. What would the fire department say? A disgusted Yochan phoned again. The chief said no. Emphatically. He had no time for euphemisms.

"Why don't we stop calling the fire department and install the cedar roof," Yochan said. "Cover it with loose tin. Then after a month or two, take it off. They'll never notice. And I doubt if they care."

I laughed but saw that Yochan meant it. Katoji, a long-time, much-decorated Shirotori fireman, nodded in agreement.

A few days later, I came across an ad in the Japan *Times* boosting asbestos paint. It said fire departments around the world loved it. Elated, I told the Takishitas I had found the answer:

Innocent of nails, sturdy ropes secure the roof on its east side.

coat the shingles with asbestos paint. It was transparent. So was
I. Yochan and his family saw through me. The dashing foreign
correspondent had the liver of a lily; he was as firm as jelly nailed
to a wall.

"Alright, I'll phone the fire chief," Yochan said, without
being asked. He dialed the number, said a few words and listened.

"The chief says he doesn't care what you coat it with," he
said. "You can use mustard, ice cream, or popcorn. It's still cedar.

Cedar burns. It is forbidden. And stop bothering him with these silly questions."

My week of indecision and inaction put me in the Takishita doghouse. Then George Inagaki, my colleague who had helped me clinch the land deal, invited Yochan and me to dinner. He said his wife's apple pie was truly epic.

Since Mao's conquest of China, I, like many other American correspondents, became a China watcher reporting from Hong Kong, then Tokyo. I already owed George a good deal professionally and personally, and would not have been able to conclude the Great Peak land transaction without him. And now, by the sheerest coincidence, he resolved the roof problem.

His boast about his wife's apple pie was an understatement. I had not had its equal since my Maine boyhood. Over dinner and afterward George and I discussed China at boring (to the others) length. When George asked about the minka, Yochan told him with wry humor about my adventures in thatch, tin, and cedar shingles.

"We'll never finish the minka if he doesn't find something," he said. "Something fireproof."

George smiled and led us, still holding our coffee cups, out onto his front porch. He lived in an upscale residential area of Kamakura, and the houses around him were solidly in the Western style.

"See that house to the left," he said, pointing at a white, three-story residence whose neat, black roof gave it an air of wealth and substance. "It is an imported slate composition, durable and fireproof. Something new around here."

Yochan got the neighbor's name and called on him the next day to get the address of the supplier. Within a week hundreds of

I gesture to David as we discuss the uncertain joys of owning, dismantling, moving, and rebuilding a minka.

sheets of black slate in dozens of packages were on the site. In my enthusiasm, I erroneously thought them shibui. Though they were handsome and restrained, they didn't, the Takishitas said, qualify.

The Inagaki dinner was one to remember. Mrs. Inagaki pressed an entire pie on us as we left. Ten years later, asbestos, once the darling of roof construction, was in bad odor, a menace to health. I might have had to remove it.

Orgies and Chamber Music

The black composite slate fitted itself to the transplanted minka like the slipper to Cinderella's foot. It wasn't as expensive as thatch and cost not much more than tin or cedar shingles. It was fireproof and resistant to wind and rain. Its color did not clash with the subdued hues of the Kamakura roofs. The black, in fact, gave the minka a clean, modest but elegant look. It was infinitely superior, I thought, to tin.

The best part was that it was easily nailed, by ordinary daiku-san, to the sheath of wooden boards that had been laid on the roof beams. Once they started, a couple of daiku, busily whacking away, completed the roof in three days.

After all the hassle about the roof material, there was general happiness to have the matter settled. Over the next few weeks Yochan and I raised an occasional glass to George Inagaki. In the excitement, however, few remembered that the need to shelter the workers against the rain and sun had been the reason for so much urgency. Japan has a heavy rainfall throughout the year. It is like the weather in my native Maine: sudden, squally, and unpredictable.

Actually, the carpenters could have done without the roof. With one exception, the entire period of construction was marked by one of the most delightful late springs and early summers anyone could remember. From Golden Week (the string of holidays beginning with the then emperor's birthday, April 29) until the drowsy days of June it rained only once before there was a roof.

It was the only day the hard-working Great Peak team took off. That included not only the carpenters and tobi but Yochan and Katoji on the hill and Kazu and assorted helpers in the rented house below.

Kazu and her sister arrived from Shirotori in the first wave with an enormous rice cooker and various other utensils to feed our small army of workers. She had to provide the spicy, herb-laced mountain diet that they were used to eating. They could have eaten the comparatively bland food of the region, but their morale would have sagged and their energy sapped at such a disappointing repast.

The women, and this included the faithful maid Kakeshita-san, all lent a hand to the cooking and kept the house and linen clean for the dozen or so visitors bedded down like so much cordwood on the floor of my rented house.

As work moved ahead in the interior, Yochan introduced one of the many innovations that have made him widely known among architects and decorators. While the daiku-san were still working on it, he laid old split bamboo on the inside ceilings of the small roofs encircling the minka. Then he poured wet plaster over them, which, when hardened, kept them in place and produced the pleasing illusion that snow was falling between the cracks.

He now turned his attention to the ceiling of the second floor and decided the wooden slats under the slate roof so much resembled the color of thatch it would be unnecessary to paint or cover them. It was at his insistence too that the carpenters laboriously wound new straw ropes around the roof beams to replace the old ones that for centuries had silently borne the burden of the minka's heavy thatch overcoat. The white stripes left on the blackened beams were reminders of where the original ropes had been.

The handsome living-room ceiling of smoked sasutake bamboo.

When I first saw the Nomura minka, its main first-floor ceiling was of thin wood with a scattering of split bamboo tacked to it. Before leaving Ise on that fateful day, Yochan and Katoji laboriously gathered several bundles of old split bamboo that they then cleaned and polished and brought to Kamakura. I paid 18,000 yen for them, the equivalent of $100, about four times more than I paid for the entire minka. They now found their places on the reconstituted ceiling of the new living room. Once green, over the centuries the bamboo had become the color of a lovingly rubbed Meerschaum pipe. In the afternoon light it shifted from old ivory to mahogany.

The old living-room area had been divided by a thin partition into two. It was easier to heat with a cast-iron pot-bellied stove. In the same way, a flimsy wooden wall on the north created a makeshift kind of kitchen. These areas were practical but architecturally troubling. I decided to relocate the kitchen to a new northeast extension and sacrifice warmth in winter for the integrity of a large, unobstructed living room. We suffered fourteen years of chilly discomfort because of this decision but never regretted it. Once all the obstructions had been removed, a room of noble proportions—thirty-two feet long, sixteen feet wide, and twelve feet high—was revealed.

One entered the revived minka through a northern entranceway or *genkan* of pounded earth. Japanese custom insisted that shoes be removed and slippers substituted before stepping up onto the wide boards of the living room. Centuries of slippered and stockinged feet had polished them to a high brownish shine. Gazing at the handsomely restored living room, I wondered how this could be the same unappealing minka I had seen, and so much disliked, two years before.

The second floor posed a different problem. It had been used for sericulture, raising and keeping silkworms to produce raw silk, a major cottage industry in Japan until only a few years ago. The worms were kept on a platform made of boards placed on shoulder-high beams. There they happily munched mulberry leaves, their food of choice, without which they wouldn't produce silk. The carpenters had the beams ready to use again, but since they would have made it almost impossible to walk erect on the second floor, Yochan and I agreed they could be discarded or used somewhere else.

Without the silkworm loft the second floor became a vast, unencumbered room framed by the eight pairs of roof beams and the thin narrow strips of wood supporting the slate roof whose light straw color gave the illusion of thatch. This unintended deception gave me, plagued as I was by the thatch dilemma, a wry sense of partial satisfaction.

The central pillar and its massive beam-branches under the ceiling

Getting to the second floor posed a problem. In the Ise incarnation one climbed a steep ladder in the cold, dark genkan entrance. I decided this was too dicey for me to negotiate. Yochan had the daiku-san cut a hole in the living-room ceiling and knocked together a wide, wooden stairway large enough even for me. It looked as old as the original minka.

Visitors gasping at the vastness of the second floor were quick to advise how it could be used. Some suggested it be converted into a gymnasium or a ping-pong hall. The more Freudian proposed orgies. Yochan liked the idea of chamber music. I compromised, favoring orgies and chamber music. In fact, we decided to leave it as it was, a reasonable facsimile of what, without silkworms, it had been.

The second-story floor was easy. Since I didn't have the money to finish it, loose boards were laid on the beams and that was that. Getting around on them proved precarious: I didn't attempt it.

Little by little the outlines of a home, as contrasted to a house, began to appear amidst all the hammering and sawing. The walls had not been built, but the floors were at last being laid, much to my relief; I had taken a couple of nasty falls walking like a tightrope artist on the slippery, bare floor beams. I just wasn't as nimble as Yochan and the daiku-san.

A Loveable American

The improvement wrought by a little dusting and some brisk shining had already begun to transform my jaundiced view of this pile I had so unwillingly bought. Removal of the silkworm shelves on the second floor and the partitions on the first had revealed the old folk house as it must have been the day it was built, more than two hundred years before. I was beginning to think more charitably of the Takishitas as the minka gradually returned to life—its early life, not the more recent one of divided rooms and bare electric light bulbs. I understood the Nomuras' need for warmth and light, but, ever the romantic, I yearned for the original. Yochan had a more realistic view of existence, and he agreed when I proposed to place a sofa, easy chairs, and a tea table at one end of the living room and my 200-year-old lacquered Chinese dining table, a Hong Kong acquisition, at the other. If I had really wanted authenticity, I would have squatted on the floor as the Nomuras and their ancestors had done for as long as anyone could remember.

Yochan encouraged my desire for comfort over verisimilitude. He did not insist that a box-like floor fireplace, called an *irori*, become the living room's center as it had in the Nomura period. It was an authentic bit of folk art with its wooden grill, pot hangers, and decorated-bamboo teapot holder, but it gave off little heat and much smoke. The smoke had curled up from the irori over the centuries through the cracks in the second floor and an opening in the roof. I was grateful that it had smoked the pillars, beams, floors, and bamboo to such an agreeable color, but I preferred more modern heating arrangements less likely to darken the lungs.

It was while making these decisions to retain the best of the old minka, combined with a touch of modern comfort, that Yochan disclosed how he planned to convert the forbidding old Nomura minka from caterpillar into butterfly, beast into beauty. He began by having the entrance face north rather than south, as it had in Ise. In doing so he violated *feng shui*, the Chinese belief that good luck blessed a house facing in the right direction. What the transplanted minka lost by this defiance of the spirits it gained in practical advantage. The entire north wall, perforated before by a couple of tiny windows, now faced south. Yochan turned it into a wall of glass with ceiling-to-floor sliding doors on one side and half-length ones on the other. It was a brilliant solution to the cold, damp, and gloom of the original. Light and sunshine poured into the living room, illuminating the rich, dark colors of the interior. Seen through the glass panels the trees, town, and ocean beyond looked like scenes from a Japanese screen, or *byobu*: a moveable feast as sun, mist, rain, snow, clouds, and darkness altered the subject and composition from hour to hour.

The living room opened up to two rooms on the north. One, in the northeast corner, had once served as a stable, the other as Nomura's reception room.

Because he was the spiritual and political head of the village, Nomura depended less on farming than his neighbors, and required less pounded earth doma space for winter chores than they did. The only two domas were the small one in the genkan and the room-sized one in the stable. What to do with it?

Working on the east dormer

I saw that it was dominated by an overhead beam of impressive size and decided it could be the top part of a large tokonoma, a display recess for scrolls. We converted the stable into a guest room floored in tatami with a ceiling of rough cedar bark (this time I didn't get the approval of the fire chief), and Yochan installed another wall of glass looking out on what became an exquisite small garden of pine, camellia, and azalea. It became my favorite room, where I would spend long hours seated on the tatami, gazing out at the garden.

The same kind of wide, old polished boards as in the living room carried over into the reception room. Nomura and his ancestors received the villagers there, gave them spiritual and practical advice, and heard their complaints and grievances.

A large room, the ceiling was of stained pine rather than split bamboo. Its northern wall, like that of the old stable, was dark and windowless. Yochan, wielding his paintbrush of light, replaced it with four more full-length sliding windows opening onto a rank and weed-filled empty field owned by an absentee landlord. I yearned to acquire it, but recognizing the slimness of my purse, put such extravagant thoughts out of my head, though they returned time and again.

The carpenters during all this time were nailing together the laths to which the white plaster of some of the walls would cling and cutting and staining the wood of others that would become the outer wall. Used to the hollow double-thickness walls of New England, I was astonished at how thin, hardly the thickness of a finger, these were. When I aired my doubts to Yochan and the daiku-san, I was told not to worry. Kamakura winters were not that bad. Houses in the north where it snowed heavily and was bitterly cold were better insulated.

The reconstruction could have stopped with the attic and the three big ground-floor rooms already described and I still would have had a house far bigger than most in Japan. But there were three other first-story rooms on the east: two for sleeping, the third housing the elaborate Nomura Buddhist altar. Shinto and Buddhism lived companionably side-by-side. These would have to be totally rebuilt rather than restored.

The Nomura minka had no indoor toilets or bath and nothing like a modern kitchen. The Nomuras and their forebears bathed outside and used outdoor toilet facilities. Recalling my own childhood two-holers and Saturday-night baths in the kitchen of my Waterville home, I could not be critical of these primitive arrangements.

Tadashi Mizoguchi applies plaster to the area above the west dormer window.

Yochan converted the two old sleeping spaces and the altar room into a separate flush toilet next to a modern bath, and a room on the northeast became my study and bedroom. A new wing on the southeast housed the kitchen.

The kitchen was small, the bath barely adequate (this would change later), and the study/bedroom a confused jumble once I had installed a bookcase, bed, typewriter (and later a computer), and chest of drawers. Because it would have been cultural sacrilege to put all these things on tatami, I installed brown wall-to-wall carpeting that matched the ceiling of small wooden beams. It was sufficiently modest to match the overall restraint of the rest of the minka.

Yochan chose to sleep on the second floor on a hastily built bed of raised tatami under the eastern eaves. Part of it was open to the sky and on occasion snow drifted onto his electric blanket, creating a mood of sweet nostalgia for Shirotori and the mountains. Weatherby called it the best part of the house.

Electric blankets would be in demand during the winter months as cold descended on the newly built minka, for I could not afford the central heating system I wanted. Instead we relied on gas delivered in large cylinders to feed the cooking stove and the large triangular gas heaters bought under the foolish impression they would, or could, warm the cavernous interior.

Kamakura is a place that prides itself on its past splendors and present culture. No unusual architectural events go unnoticed. One night Yochan and I were astonished to find a large framed photograph of the minka on the wall of our favorite tofu restaurant. The owner didn't know it was ours when he took it.

"Oh yes, you are the gaijin who has built a minka on the Great Peak," said the smiling middle-aged gentleman in the telephone company office. "What can I do for you?"

I explained I needed a telephone.

"Well," he said, "you are not exactly in a convenient location. There are no houses close to you. In fact they are rather far away. Ordinarily it would take a year, but let me see."

He turned to a colleague and said something in Japanese I couldn't catch.

"That is a striking-looking minka," he said, turning back to me. "Let's see, would two weeks be okay?"

Yochan laughed skeptically. The telephone man smiled.

"It's not a joke. I meant it," he said. "You have a choice of two numbers. Which one do you want?"

A week later three young men in telephone-company uniform appeared and planted a thirty-foot pole at the southeast corner of the small concrete garage Uncle Nakaichi had built and strung a line into the minka. I was in business. (The good will persisted. Nine years later, when a second house appeared on the Great Peak next to mine, the telephone and power people agreed to run their lines to it behind the minka to avoid obstructing my southern view.)

The generosity of the Nomuras also continued. Not content with having given me their home, they now threw in the old American clock that had hung on its walls for as long as they could remember. Powered by a spring and pendulum, its crudely built, simply carved wooden case and the Roman numerals on its worn face suggested it was of great age.

Katoji brought it down from Shirotori one rainy day, carrying it up the hill cradled in his arms after the taxi driver refused to deliver him to the door. Presenting it to me, he did not reveal the surprise it contained.

Bowled over by this new evidence of the Nomura kindness, I hesitated a while to remove it from its newspaper wrapping. Yochan pounded a nail into the stairway wall, hooked the clock to it, and set the pendulum in motion.

"Not so fast!" cried Katoji. "John-san, take a look in the pendulum box and tell me what you see."

I climbed the stairs, cautiously opened the simply ornamented glass door, and stopped the pendulum. I gaped in astonishment. Inside, against the back panel, was a colored lithograph of George Washington, resplendent in uniform with gold epaulets, clutching his three-cornered hat in his raised right hand.

How, why, or when this lithograph of the first American president and father of his country found its way into a primitive folk house in a remote Japanese village remains a mystery to this day. The Nomuras could only say they knew the clock was

American. It had always been in the minka. Was it possible that some patriotic clock maker in Massachusetts had pasted it inside, not knowing it would be sold by a Yankee trader in a strange and distant land? Though the minka had been built forty-two years before the American Declaration of Independence, the clock, whatever its age, could not have entered a long-closed Japan until after 1858, when trade with the United States first began.

It represented yet another link between myself, the Nomuras, and Takishitas. Though it had to be wound periodically and sometimes didn't run, it was a daily, visible reminder of the love they freely gave me, a foreigner.

I also became the recipient of affection from an unexpected quarter: the daiku-san. They began rightly by doubting my devotion to minkas and ended, after many long and liquid lunches and dinners, thinking me a rather lovable gaijin. Since foreigners are more tolerated than admired in rural Japan, this was progress. Besides, they hadn't met many others.

I took them to the Foreign Correspondents' Club where they admired the photo of me standing beside Mao Tse-tung and wrestled with knives and forks. But the most successful meals were Japanese, cooked by Kakeshita-san or Kazu in the rented house. There the atmosphere was genial, the beer, whiskey, and sake abundant, and the food to their liking. After marveling at my ability to wield chopsticks, they watched in disbelief as I wolfed down raw fish, seaweed, sticky potatoes, fermented soybeans, and glutinous rice with the best of them. They thought gaijin, besides being strangely red nosed, red haired, and descended from red devils, incapable of such feats. There was much in the way of misunderstanding to separate us, but we found common ground at the dinner table. The alcohol loosened their tongues and they talked of their wives and children. After innumerable toasts, they sang Japanese songs of love, war, and sadness. At the height of their sake-induced enthusiasm, they flung their arms around me and opined that foreigners weren't all bad.

In the final days, I was alarmed to find Yochan, usually so cheerful and upbeat, now moody, withdrawn, and silent when questioned. Twenty-two, just out of university, he had been confronted with a challenge most adults would have recoiled at accepting.

He had to take a self-taught crash course in minka construction, supervise the timbers' transfer to Kamakura, choreograph the arrival on the scene of various workmen, make a thousand small decisions on what to do and when to do it, buy the extra timber as the need arose, and carry on a continuing dialogue with Miwa, Sumi, Katoji, and Kazu. As if these burdens were not heavy enough, he had to shoulder the additional weight of interpreting everything they spoke to me, and I to them. His English then was halting and when it came to technical building terms he sometimes was stumped. It was no wonder he tottered on the edge of mental and physical exhaustion.

"I need a vacation," he said. "I've got to get away from all this."

I agreed.

We had talked for some time about the possibility of his doing graduate studies in the United States, and I asked through a friend in New York what universities were the most promising. The reply did not help: most required a year of remedial English before he could take any serious courses. In the end, he decided to take a trip around the world on the sound, if unproven, premise that it might prove more educational.

Money, which worried me inordinately when I didn't have it, held no similar terror for Yochan. Noting that my own financial resources now were almost at the vanishing point after borrowing from both the AP and a friend to pay the remaining $5,000 of the $20,000 I owed for the house and land, I asked how he intended to finance this ambitious journey.

"I'll hitchhike," he said with serene confidence. "All I need is a simple place to sleep and a crust of bread and cheese to eat."

Thus it was that in late June 1967, he embarked on a Soviet passenger ship bound for Khabarovsk from Yokohama on the first leg of an eighteen-month adventure that would take him via the Trans-Siberian Railway to Moscow and then to thirty-four countries in Europe, the Middle East, North Africa, and the Americas.

Katoji, Kazu, his brother and sister, and I saw him off in Yokohama. The prospect of the travels ahead buoyed him and he was once more the same high-spirited, optimistic youth I had grown to know and love. He needed the optimism: besides his ticket, some money from Kazu and Katoji, and promise of more from me whenever he needed it, he was penniless.

"Don't worry about the water," he said to me as he waited to board the ship. "I've talked to the committee chairman and he says the electric connections will be finished in three days. The system then will be functional."

The Takishitas and I waved frantically at Yochan's dwindling figure as the ship pulled out to sea. There were tears in Katoji's eyes.

"Will we ever see him again?" he asked.

I put one arm on his shoulder and assured him we would.

Katoji, Kazu, and Yochan beam from a nearly finished window.

Three days later, as Yochan predicted, water from the small well surged upward with such force it burst a pipe a few yards short of the three-legged storage tank. The plumbers swiftly applied a tourniquet of plastic to the wound and the minka's lifeblood splashed into the kitchen sink. I gazed at the clear, pure stream gushing out of the faucet and recalled with a sigh the months of anxiety and struggle by Yochan and the Takishitas to revitalize the old Nomura minka. Now with this cheapest and most necessary of nature's gifts, it had truly embarked on a new life.

As summer reached its peak and declined into long, sleepy days of autumn, rattling around in its echoing chambers, I began to feel the first real stirrings of affection for this great wooden pile I had once despised. My feelings for it—and for him—grew as Yochan's absence lengthened. I began to see it not only as an interesting building architecturally, but as a shelter under which two centuries of humans had lived out their varied lives. They crowded into my dreams, their boots muddy from the watery rice paddies, their stockinged feet polishing the wide floor boards, their gnarled hands stretched out to the warmth of the smoky flames leaping out of the irori.

I saw them at work in the doma, weaving baskets, making pickles for the long winter, and repairing farm utensils and worn clothes. Turning on my side I saw these same tired farmers and their wives, backs bent from too much stooping in the rice paddies, dressed in summer *yukata* and *kimono* for the Obon Festival, sweeping and watering the graves, and dancing the whole night through to honor and humor the dead.

There too was Nomura, wearing his threadbare silk jacket and stiff black hat, waving a branch of the sakaki tree and scattering white squares of paper at weddings and land- and house-dedication ceremonies.

Awaking, I tried to piece together the meaning of my life in Japan, to discover its significance and where it was leading me. I found it astonishing that I, a questioning, often critical journalist, a lapsed Roman Catholic, the descendent of easy-going, wine-loving French men and women, should feel so much at home in such a strange country whose language I had only barely mastered and whose thinking often baffled me.

The curious thing was that I did not find the Japanese either strange or exotic. They certainly were unique, just as every race is. And their culture, though influenced by contact with China, bore the unmistakable mark of their own genius. Their houses of worship were different from those in Europe and America, but the constancy and sincerity of their faith were the same.

The Takishitas and the rough, hard-working people in the countryside I met through them persuaded me that humans basically are good, but can be corrupted by war and greed. I discovered that the basic building block of Japan was, and still is, the family, and that its economic success rests squarely on this unshakeable foundation. I was living proof that the family, especially in Japan, can do the impossible if it is motivated by love, even love for a gaijin, the once-hated American enemy.

Whatever I may have thought of it in the beginning, this old Japanese folk house now dominated my life. I would never again think the same or feel the same as I had before acquiring it. Not only was it the home I had never had, but, more significantly, it had become the symbol of my relationship to the Takishitas. Tall and stately on a hilltop overlooking the capital of its ancient Minamoto enemy, it had shrugged off the dust and romance of history and now, reborn in the twentieth century, had begun a new and unpredictable existence with a different master: a blond, blue-eyed, somewhat plump, over-awed native of Maine, the most distant of American states from Japan.

Sitting on the grass terrace in front of my minka, balancing a dry martini in one hand, I surveyed the emptiness of the Great Peak and yearned for Yochan to return so we could begin living among the neighbors who, now that water had been found, were sure to come.

At last, a house of my own

Book Two

Beauty has power to disarm the raging barbarian; there is no greater security against violence and injury than beauty and dignity.

—LEON BATTISTA ALBERTI

Feel Poor!

Yochan's journey to Russia, Europe, the Middle East, and America came at a critical, formative period in his young life.

He was a likeable, pleasant, easy-going country boy, thrilled to be in Tokyo and at Waseda, when I met him. Fascinated by the large, outgoing, self-confident Americans who thronged the emerging metropolis, he never in his wildest dreams thought he would meet one.

During his university years, through me, he met not only other Americans but the various other foreigners—teachers, mostly, and other correspondents—of my acquaintance.

All this time he was becoming less provincial and more international. His English, barely understandable at first, became fluent. He immersed himself in Western things—Mozart and Beethoven, spaghetti and peanut butter and jelly sandwiches, American movies and television programs (they helped improve his English).

The minka reconstruction was another step in his education. It plunged him into a position of leadership unusual for one so young. He found himself the head man of a project that required constant attention to detail, an undertaking complicated by the fact that it was being built for me, a foreigner. His involvement in all its aspects—hourly supervision, interpreting, acting as a gofer, helping make decisions, and assisting the carpenters—left him exhausted but also older, wiser, and more confident than before.

In leaving Japan so soon after granting my wish for a home of my own he began what essentially was a search for his own identity. He was torn between town and country, wished to be part of one as well as the other. The old minka, with its roots in the mountains, resolved this tug-of-war within him. Its almost rural setting on a green hilltop within commuting distance to Tokyo partly satisfied both urges. Now he was about to dip a toe into international waters to see how the West, the Middle East, and Africa compared with Japan, for whose history and culture he felt a fierce pride.

His voyage of discovery was done on the cheap, by ship, train, hitch-hiking; he couldn't afford to fly. He marveled at the Kremlin in Moscow, was overwhelmed by the treasures of St. Petersburg, marched up the Champs-Élysées in Paris with French students demonstrating for reforms, slept in the desert in Libya, froze on trains in Turkey, sold his blood in Kuwait, found romance on the beaches in Spain, spent two months brushing up his English in Cambridge, sailed on the *Queen Elizabeth* to New York, visited my family in Maine, and attended the Republican convention in Miami.

Yochan returned to Kamakura from Honolulu deeply tanned and wearing a pineapple hat. He was glad, he said, to have gone and even more to be back.

Not long afterward he took the oral part of the bar exam and passed, but he failed the written, a minefield of tricky questions designed to discourage. Of 15,000 who took it that year, only 500 passed. Lawyers are few, lawsuits rare, and justice glacially slow in Japan.

Now convinced he didn't want to be a lawyer, he got a job with a travel agency, took a Rotary group on a tour of the South

Pacific and Australia, and quit in six months. His was too free
a spirit to be tied down by the "escalator system," which rewards
longevity and punishes imagination and ability.

In this mood, I sat down with him to discuss what he might
do next. Yochan spoke of his delight in the Japanese art he had
seen in the museums of Europe and America. He recalled that
his grandfather had been a collector of Japanese antiques.

"What about going into the antique business?" I asked.

"I've been thinking of that," he replied. "But how?"

I remembered David Kidd, an American friend I had known
in Peking. He now was a successful antique dealer in Ashiya, near
Kobe, living in a three-hundred-year-old mansion transplanted
from Shikoku. Contacted by phone, he agreed to see Yochan.
During a week of discussions with him and his Japanese
partner, Morimoto, Yochan learned the ropes of successful
sales and collecting.

"To be a successful collector," David told him, "you must
remember to feel poor when you buy. Then doubt the desirability
and authenticity of the item before you buy it. After that, doubt
again. Once you are convinced, feel poor again. Sell at a fixed
price. No bargaining, a la Chinese. Stay thin. People don't trust
a fat dealer. And never make a refund; urge the customer to take
something else in trade."

Armed with these nine commandments, Yochan returned
to Kamakura just in time to bid me farewell. It was the spring of
1971 and I had just returned from covering the U.S. table tennis
team's tour of China, a historic breakthrough, which signaled the
end of the Sino-American Cold War. I was going to New York for
four months to do a book and a China documentary for AP. If he
finished the minka's second floor, I told him, he could start his

antique business there. He did, and he called it "The House of Antiques."

During my absence, he festooned the second floor with Boy's Day banners, crudely painted celebrations of samurai life, circular saws, wooden bowls, *usus* (hollow tree trunks in which New Year's rice is pounded), and dozens of big and small porcelain sake bottles. It was a modest beginning, financed by the money and tips he had saved from the tourist agency. But he was his own boss, taking orders from no one, not even me. Recognizing that the House of Antiques was as much a declaration of independence as a business, I carefully refrained from interfering.

Yochan bought a small van and began scouring the countryside once a month for antiques picked up in smoke-filled auction rooms or occasionally bought from individuals and families. His earliest enthusiasms were for blue-and-white Japanese and Chinese porcelains, an eager interest he communicated to his audience. He spent more than two months a year on the road on these buying trips. Clients came by telephone appointment because the minka was hard to find. This gave him time to improve his collection and give lectures on Japanese art and antiques to embassies, women's clubs, military posts, and service organizations.

The originally unwanted minka had persuaded me to spend the rest of my career, perhaps my life, under its sheltering eaves. And now Yochan, surrounded by his colorful banners and porcelains on the second floor, had also committed himself. Yochan's choice for his life's work could not have been a happier one. The objects he brought to the minka from all over Japan, and from many ages, enhanced its beauty and authenticity. They were, in a way, part of its heritage.

Gradually, as he enlarged his collection, the old minka became a museum of Japanese handicrafts and art. When it rose on the Great Peak, it was as devoid of art and artifacts as it had been in Ise. My only souvenirs of years in China were a three-color glaze Tang statue, the dining-room table, and an intricately woven imperial picnic basket, which I brought out of China from the ping-pong trip the previous April. The Takishitas had given me a *tansu* set of drawers, three lovely Kutani bowls, and an old screen.

Within months the artistic famine turned into a feast as Yochan enlarged and refined his collection to include both colored and blue-and-white Imari porcelains, Buddhist statues, Japanese and Chinese tea tables, paper *andon* lanterns, *hibachi* sake and tea warmers, incense burners, scrolls, paintings, screens, clay pots, and a wide variety of furniture.

All these objects, spilling over into the living-room below, contributed to my education in Japanese art and culture. Yochan described their origins and the techniques that went into their creation, whetting an interest that, until then, I had neglected. I left sometimes on month-long trips to China or Southeast Asia and on my return exclaimed over the acquisitions Yochan had made. I had the sensation of living not only in a museum, but one whose exhibitions, changing periodically, provided a moveable feast, a continuing delight.

In the midst of all this, always searching for an apt quotation, I came across one from Elizabeth Ammons's introduction to Edith Wharton's *Summer*, which I showed to Yochan.

"The preservation of art and architecture created by our predecessors is one way," it said, "in which we keep with us a sense of continuity with the people who came before."

It could have been referring to Yochan, the old minka, and to a lesser degree, me.

White Ants

The day the renovated minka was basically finished, Yochan and I decided to spend the night in it before electricity was installed. We wanted to recapture the mood of 1734 when it was built, sans light, sans television, sans radio; in a word, without any of the utilities twenty-first-century man cannot live without.

When we arrived that night, armed with pajamas and toothbrushes, we found to our dismay the television set inside, hooked up to the portable gasoline-powered generator outside. We had not told Katoji of our fantasy. He assumed we would want the comforts of this age rather than that of a long-vanished one.

"Damn," I said. "Let's take it out."

"No need to do that," said Yochan, more practical. "Just leave it there, but don't turn it on."

We left it.

After several hours of candle light in the dark, we decided that life two centuries earlier must have been monumentally boring. It became evident why farmers in any age before that of electricity went to bed early and got up early. Aside from sex— and how long does that last?—there was nothing much to do.

Boredom won out.

"Okay," I said. "Turn it on."

Channel One, the semi-public NHK network, lit up the screen. We watched in disbelief as the camera panned through the living room of a massive minka like the one in which we were sitting.

"Beautiful!" exclaimed Yochan.

Whatever he intended to say next died in mid-sentence. Before our horrified eyes, the minka's huge beams, and those of a succession of others, collapsed, one after the other, like broken chopsticks. It was, I thought, like Poe's *Fall of the House of Usher*.

"This is what happens," said the announcer in a voice of doom, "when *shiro ari* invade wooden houses. They feast on them."

"What," I asked, "are shiro ari?"

"They're termites," said Yochan. "What we call 'white ants.'"

For a full hour, we watched in horror as these industrious little insects nibbled through the pillars and beams to extract the sugary bits they obediently carried to their waiting queen.

"Have you ever seen anything so ugly?" I asked. "She's like the mad queen in *Alice in Wonderland*."

When the program ended, I raised the obvious question. I knew little or nothing about termites.

"Do we have any?" I asked.

"I don't think so," said Yochan. "We knew about them in the country. Shiro ari love low, wet places. We're on a hill and winds are fairly strong. They keep the ground dry."

Yochan wasn't taking any chances, however. The next day he asked the carpenters to cut a dozen new air vents above the foundation.

"That should do it," he said.

It didn't prevent me from having nightmares in which hideous-looking termite queens chased me around the bed.

Two years later, not long after Yochan had returned from his trip abroad, I came across a small pile of wood dust under a beam in the tatami guest room.

"What does it look like to you?" I asked Yochan.

He examined the pile closely.

"It does look like shiro ari," he said. "We'd better do something about it."

Some time after the terrifying TV program, I had come across the newspaper advertisement of a large firm specializing in insect extermination and squirreled it away in a desk drawer for possible future use. But Yochan had a candidate of his own, a freelancer from Yokohama. Let's call him Ari-san.

He was short, red faced, and serious. I left for Tokyo after the introductions and Yochan continued the discussion over a bowl of noodles, the weapon of choice in all Japanese negotiations.

The story Yochan told me that night intrigued and alarmed me. Ari was no ordinary exterminator. He agreed to tackle the termites head on. That was reassuring. His background, related to Yochan at length, was not.

In World War II he was a sergeant in the Aleutians, off Alaska, the last survivor of an Imperial Army company engaged by the Americans. His comrades had either died in battle or committed *hara kiri*, suicide by disembowelment. It was considered a disgrace to be captured by the enemy. Death was preferable to dishonor.

Wounded and unconscious, Sgt. Ari awoke to find himself a prisoner of the dreaded Americans. But instead of killing or torturing him, his captors were attempting to save his life. He lay on a cot bed, his veins connected to dripping fluids, which kept him alive. The Americans were a short distance away, gathered around a campfire.

Sgt. Ari felt neither gratitude nor sympathy for these softhearted soldiers. Fumbling at his belt, he felt a single hand grenade, pulled the pin, and hurled it into the fire. In the confusion after the explosion, which certainly must have taken a toll in men killed and wounded, he escaped.

Rejoining a new unit, he became a guard in a camp for American prisoners. At war's end, expatriated to Japan, he was tried and convicted of cruelty to them and served seven years in a war crimes prison.

He told Yochan that when he got out, his outlook on life changed.

"I felt remorse for what I had done," he said. "To repay my debt to society, I became a pest exterminator. In that way I make life for my fellow humans easier and safer."

Yochan told him about the NHK shiro ari documentary.

"I was a consultant on that project," he said.

He once was invited to inspect the imperial villa in Hayama, not far from Kamakura. It teemed, he said, with termites. Asked to get rid of them, he jotted down the estimated cost. The humorless representative of the Imperial Household Agency (Kunaicho) was not amused. He frostily reminded the ex-sergeant that it was a privilege to serve the emperor. Payment was out of the question.

"I was ready to lay down my life for the emperor," he replied, "but that was wartime. Things have changed. I have to make a living. No money, no work."

A few years later nature did the job he had refused to do. Fire destroyed the villa, and with it, the imperial ants.

I was dubious about hiring an ex–war criminal no matter how humanitarian. But Yochan insisted.

Ari showed up the next day dressed like a surgeon about to perform a particularly difficult operation. From head to toe he was a symphony in white: white cap, jacket, trousers, socks, and shoes.

I could only guess at his underwear. To complete the medical look, he carried a black bag.

Before getting down to business, he produced a photo album that recorded his numerous conquests of the shiro ari. Then he pulled a glass jar from his bag and extracted a queen termite. It was repulsively arrogant. I expected it to cry out, "Off with her head! Off with her head!"

After that Ari-san slowly paced around the tatami, then, armed with a flashlight, pulled up one of the floor panels and descended, like Orpheus, into the crawlspace below.

For fifteen minutes Yochan and I waited as he rummaged around beneath the floor. At the end of that time he emerged, a triumphant look on his face, brandishing a sliver of wood on which crawled several live termites.

"That's it!" he cried. "You indeed have shiro ari. These came off the rotting wood under the floor. Now let's find out where they come from."

He fished out of his black bag a shiny metal instrument resembling a portable cassette player. Placed against the wall or a beam, he explained, it amplified the footfalls of the termites as they joyously raced to satisfy the queen's insatiable craving for wood sugar.

"Aha, that's it," he said once more. "They are moving from the crawl space through the beams to the wooden horse trough outside. The queen is there."

The trough in question, a gift from Katoji, was large and old and filled with water. It seemed an ideal palace for a queen termite.

The gadget fascinated me. I reached for it but Ari-san resisted. I insisted, placed it against one of the beams, and listened intently. It was the one Ari-san had, in a manner of speaking, wiretapped.

"Funny, I don't hear anything," I said, disappointed.

Impatiently Ari-san took it from me and listened. "You are too clumsy," he said, annoyed. "You don't know how to use it. The least noise freezes them in their tracks."

I felt as though he had gone through Alice's mirror into a world that was not what it seemed. I kept my thoughts to myself.

Ari-san added up some figures and announced that for $1,000 he would rid the minka of its termites as well as any snakes, scorpions, centipedes, spiders, or caterpillars unlucky enough to inhale the deadly poisons he intended to pour into the immense tent with which he would cover the house. It would be uninhabitable, he said, for five days.

I nodded. It would strain my budget, still recovering from the purchase of the minka and the land, but the alternative was unacceptable. I recalled the collapsing NHK minkas and shuddered.

"We will call you in a few days," Yochan said.

Two days later, after dinner, Yochan announced: "I think I'll take a look down there."

He took a flashlight, pulled up the tatami mat, and jumped into the crawl space. Three minutes later he came out.

"Guess what I found," he said.

He held up the glass jar with the ugly queen and a half-dozen lively termites inside.

"And in case you're interested," he continued, "there isn't a single rotten floor beam. They're all as solid as when we laid them."

The pathetic truth was that Ari-san needed money. Business was slow. There weren't any termites, so he supplied them from the glass jar and placed them on the rotten sliver he had brought with him. He made the mistake of leaving the evidence behind.

Yochan phoned him and said the project would have to wait; I was off on a trip to Australia. The second part was true. Ari-san got the message. He didn't ask when I would be back.

A week later, my experts appeared, tapped the beams with a hammer, and said the minka was as sound as a nut.

The Evil Eye

During Yochan's travels abroad, our maid Kakeshita-san cooked for me, kept the minka tidy, did the shopping, and saw that I was dressed in clean, well-pressed clothes. I communicated with her in my basic Japanese—she spoke no English. But there were few misunderstandings. She was a small, quiet woman of great dignity, never inclined to gossip or engage in small talk. An American friend introduced her to me in 1959, not long after I had arrived in Tokyo.

Kakeshita-san came from a distinguished family. Her uncle was Baron Kiichiro Hiranuma, briefly wartime prime minister, a leading rightist responsible for Japan's alliance with Hitler and Mussolini. She was a superb cook. When I asked her to serve lobster, she reeled off eight different ways of preparing this Maine delicacy. Her skills, if anything, had improved in Kamakura.

Since Yochan and I commuted to university and the office five days a week, she ordinarily had time to spare. Kakeshita-san missed Hoagy Carmichael. Shortly before the move from the rented house to the minka, this much-loved little black dog was bitten on the nose by a mosquito and contracted heartworms. Once bright and lively, she became listless and silent. Yochan had to take her to the veterinarian to put her to sleep. When he returned from this sad errand, he drank a half bottle of whiskey, sat on the floor, and cried. I had never before seen him drunk.

The minka was larger and more difficult to manage than the rented house across town. Though she was a splendid cook, Kakeshita-san had difficulty with the housework. I decided to hire an all-around maid to give her a helping hand. (Living in Japan at that time was, for Americans, not only affordable but cheap. The dollar fetched 360 yen, more than three times what it does today. Salaries were low. To have two or three servants was not unusual.)

Kakeshita-san's new assistant, whom we shall call Suzuki-san, a petite, bustling bundle of energy from the neighboring town of Ofuna, could not have been more socially different. She was a country girl and had blunt country manners. Where Kakeshita-san was reserved, often silent, Suzuki-san burbled. She was a chatterbox, always cheerful, always busy.

She came from Northern Honshu, where the winters are bone-chillingly cold and last six months. Married to the son of a prosperous farmer before the war, she had four children, two boys and two girls. Called to the colors, her husband died, still young, in China. When his ashes returned in a box covered with white cloth, the drama of her life began.

She got caught up in a bitter quarrel with her husband's parents over who should possess them.

"He was our son. We are entitled to them!" they cried.

"He was my husband, father of my children!" she exclaimed. "They are mine!"

Unable to bend Suzuki-san's proud and unwavering will, the parents now resorted to a cruel stratagem. They announced they would stop feeding the little family until the ashes were handed over. Impetuosity was one of Suzuki-san's weaknesses. She acted too often in hot blood. We will never know whether they intended to withhold food indefinitely. Surely no one with the smallest shred of compassion would do such a thing to one's own grandchildren.

Suzuki-san didn't wait to find out. She packed her bags, including the ashes, and left on the next train, and she never saw her in-laws again.

She settled in Ofuna, near Kamakura, and there discovered she had a green thumb. She grew perfect vegetables and industrial crops in a borrowed garden, making enough to keep her small family alive and, indeed, prosper over the years. She never remarried.

Before coming to my minka, she had been a part-time hospital worker, cleaning the wards and massaging the patients. She missed cooking for her children, taking care of the small details of their lives. I was impressed by her eagerness, good humor, and neat appearance. There had been earlier candidates who smoked, drank, or were slovenly.

Suzuki-san's eyes widened when she saw the Great Peak minka. It reminded her of the farmhouse she had lived in so long before.

"She," I thought, "is a gem. She has enthusiasm, isn't afraid to work for a foreigner, and has a great sense of humor. She has me laughing much of the time. I hope she gets along with Kakeshita-san."

Kakeshita-san kept her thoughts to herself. She accepted this brash, new assistant with her usual restraint while Suzuki-san, recognizing her social superiority, treated her with outward respect. But she soon began plotting to gain mastery of the household. She did not tip her hand at once. She was too shrewd for that. Instead, she began a campaign to win me over. Each day, for the first two weeks, she brought me a gift. Instead of being grateful, I was embarrassed. I had been in Japan long enough to know that gifts are rigidly structured. The recipient must respond with something half its value. Until he does, he labors under a heavy obligation, an *on* he must discharge. Foreigners, knowing no better, generally are excused from this formal dance of duty. But it nonetheless bothered me.

She arrived one day with a gift more ornate than the others, an elaborate *Fuji musume* doll in a glass case, much admired by many Japanese. I rebelled. It had been in her family for years. She was taken aback when I politely but firmly refused it.

"I'm sorry," I said, "but it is valuable and you should keep it."

"But," she sputtered, "it will give the house a feminine touch."

I smiled. "I really don't need a feminine touch," I replied. "You and Kakeshita-san are quite enough. And, although I really appreciate them, you must stop giving me gifts. They put me under an obligation that makes me uncomfortable."

This was language she understood. She bowed her head. After that there were no more gifts.

Life in the old minka flowed smoothly for the next few months without incident. Then Suzuki-san began to complain to me that Kakeshita-san wasn't doing her job.

"She's too slow," she said. "It takes her all day to do anything."

I explained this was why she had been hired, to shoulder some of the housework, and added, "I'm completely happy with her. She's family."

That silenced her for a while. Then one day she entered the north room, used as a bedroom, without knocking. It was morning, and a houseguest, a British professor, was asleep inside. She saw him and burst out of the room.

"You didn't tell me someone was in there!" she shouted at Kakeshita-san. "I went in without knocking. You've made me lose face."

Face in Japan means dignity, prestige, self-respect. Losing it is a serious business. Dumbfounded, the gentle Kakeshita-san replied quietly: "You should have asked."

"No, it's your fault. Don't try to get around it. You're too old to work here. You should quit."

Present at this exchange, I watched to see how Kakeshita-san would react. Beneath the silky exterior there was tempered steel. I had once seen another woman prostrate herself full length on the floor begging her forgiveness after a perceived insult.

She drew herself up to her full five feet two inches.

"It was your responsibility to find out if there was anyone in the room before you entered," she said. "That is only common sense. If anyone goes, it won't be me."

They glared at each other. I tried to dismiss the incident as not worth fighting over. They ignored me.

Later, speaking through Yochan, just back from his overseas trip, I told Kakeshita-san, "It was a silly thing for Suzuki-san to say. You were absolutely right. If you wish, I'll find someone else."

She declined. But in the weeks that followed she appeared to have lost her will to go on working. During that time, the two women ignored each other. The situation was intolerable.

"It's true," she told me, "Suzuki was right. I don't have the energy any more to do anything. I need a rest. I hope you don't mind."

I was aghast at the thought of losing her. She had been with me eleven years. She was, in her unobtrusive way, part of my life. I tried to persuade her to stay, promised to replace Suzuki with someone more acceptable to her. She wouldn't budge.

"I really am tired," she said. "I've enjoyed working for you but my family in Tokyo needs me. May I come back to see you once in a while?"

Kakeshita-san represented to me the best of Japan: polite, industrious, dignified, thoughtful, loyal. I wanted to give in to my Latin emotions and embrace her, but clearly that was out of the question. Instead, I bowed gravely, wiping away a tear.

"Of course," I said. "We must continue to be friends. Come whenever you wish."

I gave her an envelope containing cash and together with Yochan saw her off at the station. Her devotion to me never flagged. We kept in touch for years. She visited often and remembered Yochan and me with gifts of oranges, grapes, or persimmons in season.

Suzuki-san showed no remorse.

"Good riddance," she muttered under her breath, then turned away when she saw the ominous clouds gathering on my face.

The moment Kakeshita-san had gone, Suzuki-san became as busy as a bee, flying around the house, preparing and cooking meals, cleaning the dust out of every corner. Throughout this frenetic activity, she sang songs of her childhood. And she joked with me, but not with Yochan. In any case, he was busy laying the foundations of his antique business and had little time for small pleasantries. I had plenty.

In less than two years, she had become mistress of the Great Peak minka.

"Oh, no," she replied when Yochan suggested she needed a helper. "I can do it all by myself. I like it that way."

It soon became apparent she resented Yochan as she had Kakeshita-san. In my eyes, Yochan could do no wrong. He had built the minka against all odds, mastered English by himself, then traveled around the world alone. He was twenty-three and had many friends. But in his dealings with those working for him, he was more foreign than Japanese. He treated them fairly and was grateful for what they did, but he didn't say so often enough.

He was everything I would have wanted in a son. Ours was a bantering relationship, half amused, half serious. Yochan left me notes calling me "Mr. President" when I was head of the press club and "VCW," "veteran China watcher," the words AP used on my China stories. Our affection was flavored with humor. In the beginning, Yochan grossly spoiled me, leaping to satisfy my every whim. When I protested, weakly, Yochan grinned. "Small voice," he said, and we laughed at this recognition of my willingness to be indulged.

We were never bored with each other.

Suzuki-san next began a whispering campaign among the small number of neighbors now living on the Great Peak. She sang my virtues but painted Yochan in somber tones. Then one day she dropped her bombshell.

"Yochan has the evil eye," she whispered. It was an insidious accusation, designed to do maximum damage. A superstition shared by many Japanese, those with the evil eye are said to be able to ruin people's lives merely by staring fixedly at them. It is dangerous to make long eye-contact with someone on the train, no matter how innocently. Murder sometimes is the price one pays.

Suzuki-san's charges were so obviously ridiculous, few paid attention. Generally popular in the neighborhood, Yochan laughed when he heard about it.

"She's a simple woman," he said. "I'm sorry she feels that way. But she works hard and keeps the house clean. That's important now that my antique business is growing and more and more clients come to visit us. I need her, so I'll overlook it."

He was right. Though she was far from being the cook Kakeshita-san had been, her meals were edible. She was quick and thorough, and the minka gleamed.

She was so quick she had time on her hands, time to covet the large field south of the minka owned by an amiable farmer. Looking at it each day aroused memories of the war, the husband she had lost, and her happiness working the fields in Ofuna.

The Spoons

One day, unable to resist the temptation, Suzuki-san approached the farmer with a cake and a request. Would he be so kind as to loan her part, a small part, of the field? It would, she said, please me.

By this time, I was well known in and around the Great Peak as the gaijin who had brought water to its parched acres. The farmer almost certainly was delighted to do a favor for me. He readily assented. I had not, of course, suggested he part with even the smallest bit of his land. It would have embarrassed me to do so.

From that day, life changed for Suzuki-san. She now was reunited with an old love, the good rich earth. Rising at 5 o'clock each morning, she took the train from Ofuna to Kamakura, arriving five minutes later. Then she trudged for twenty minutes from the station and up the steep hill to the Great Peak, where she worked her tiny plot. She put in more than three hours while we slept and entered the minka at 9 AM, after we had finished breakfast.

Soon a stream of corn, tomatoes, potatoes, peas, cauliflower, radishes, lettuce, and the good lord knows what else poured from her garden. All were near perfect or perfect. She gave them to her generous benefactor, to me, and still had enough left to fill a half-ton truck for her family.

Though I was perturbed that she had received the field on false pretenses, I kept my mouth shut. I enjoyed her bounty and praised her extravagantly before guests. She responded by growing closer to me and cooler toward Yochan.

This false calm continued for several years without incident. Then one day the peace was shattered like a sudden squall on a becalmed sea. During his Russian trip, Yochan had picked up a half-dozen brass spoons for almost nothing. Because of their interesting design, we used them for dessert.

Near the end of an otherwise pleasant lunch, while Yochan and I and our guests waited for the ice cream and cherry sauce, Suzuki-san came bounding out of the kitchen.

"The spoons! The spoons!" she cried. "Four of them are missing!"

Everyone looked at her in astonishment.

I rose and followed her back into the kitchen. "*Kamaimasen. Shikataga nai*," I said. "It doesn't matter. They're worthless. Use the other spoons."

"No! No!" she said. "It's Yochan's doing. He has hidden them so you would think I stole them. He wants to get rid of me."

Yochan by now had joined us. "That's ridiculous," he said. "I don't care about the spoons. And I certainly don't want you to leave. I appreciate your work. You are a valuable part of our household."

Suzuki-san stuck her fingers in her ears.

"I don't want to hear it," she said. "I've had enough. I quit."

Within half an hour she had wrapped up all her belongings and stormed out of the house.

Foreigners are expected to be baffled by the way Japanese think. By doing so they attest to the uniqueness of the Japanese mind. But I was not alone this time: Yochan couldn't find an explanation for this strange behavior. Life in the minka had been placid for a long time. Suzuki-san had given not the smallest hint that she was about to erupt. When she did it caught us both totally off guard. For once I couldn't think of a quotation to describe the situation.

I suggested it was a plot to alienate me from Yochan and let her take over the minka.

"Maybe she's in love with you," Yochan offered. "Something Freudian. Inexplicable."

I made a face. "Maybe," I said. "Anything is possible."

Whatever the reason, Suzuki-san's departure left an immediate vacuum in the ordered life of the minka. The shopping, cooking, and cleaning fell on Yochan's shoulders. I helped a bit but was away in Tokyo most of the week. As a cook I was a disaster. It was safer to keep me away from the kitchen. We ate out a good deal.

Yochan gamely tackled the mounting challenges while keeping up with his growing antique business on the second floor. He couldn't find a satisfactory replacement, one remotely as good as Suzuki-san.

Eight months passed in this fashion, months not entirely disagreeable as I benefited from the revival of Yochan's skills in the kitchen. But Yochan was close to despair. Then, one day, he bumped into Suzuki-san in the market, asked her to come by for a cup of tea. To his surprise, she did, bringing with her a handsome, fourteen-year-old grandson. Tall and rosy-cheeked, it was his first visit to the minka. When during the conversation he learned she no longer worked for us there, he showed his disappointment. She had not told him. Yochan's haragei, his gut feeling, told him it was the moment to act.

"Please come back," he pleaded. "We need you."

She returned to work the next day.

Life in the old minka resumed its ordered way as though nothing had happened. Soon she was humming her little tunes as she cooked and tidied up. She went back to the farmer's garden and began producing those famous vegetables again.

Yochan and I pretended that everything was as before. But behind the facade ran an undercurrent of uneasiness. We were like children, fingers stuck in our ears, waiting for the firecracker to explode. For three years it didn't, and we were grateful.

Her return left Yochan free to concentrate on his antiques. If he worried at all, it was over the time she spent in the garden. It had become an obsession with her; often she didn't appear at the kitchen door until 10 AM. She seemed to have no time for the minka. He said nothing, unwilling to trigger another outburst. She was too necessary to his plans. He did not want to repeat the trauma of her departure, for whatever reason.

We were not alone during this time. Kazu and Katoji came down every so often. They treated Suzuki-san with respect. She was, after all, from the country too. They thought they knew her better than Kakeshita-san because of this.

Katoji couldn't stand clutter and disorganization. In the cavalry he was a supply officer and had to keep accurate accounts, or else. In Kamakura he couldn't be happy without doing something. If he wasn't packing loose objects like paper and sticks into tidy bundles, which was highly appreciated, he was pruning the roses to within inches of their lives, which wasn't. He cut back one of the *bonsai* dwarf trees so savagely it gave up the struggle and died, piteously.

One afternoon, rummaging behind a *kuruma tansu*, a chest of drawers on wheels, he came across a futon cover.

"What's this?" he asked, shaking the dust out of it. "How did this get here?"

It was a rhetorical question. He didn't really care how it got there. But it was the spark that finally ignited the firecrackers.

"Yochan did it!" shouted Suzuki-san. "He wants John-san to blame me for misplacing it. It's an excuse to let me go!"

It was a replay of the Russian brass spoons scenario.

Yochan and I reacted with dismay and disbelief. We were no nearer to understanding her this time than we were then. We tried, half-heartedly, to talk her out of leaving, secretly relieved to see her go. Waiting for the explosion had been nearly as exhausting as the explosion itself. We were tired of living on the slopes of this hyperactive volcano.

Three days after she had gone back to Ofuna, I felt a touch of remorse. I wrote her a letter of recommendation.

"I am sorry you had to leave," I wrote in the usual insincere preamble. "But we wish to give you a letter you can show your next employer saying you were hard-working and honest."

It went on in that vein.

Receiving the letter a few days later, she read the first paragraph and flew to the telephone. Yochan answered.

"I've read the letter," she said triumphantly. "John-san is sorry I left. So I've decided to come back."

Yochan's face fell. I was aghast.

"Let's settle this, once and for all," I said. "It's my fault. I should have let well enough alone. Tell her she can come back for a three day trial period."

She appeared two days later at the kitchen door smiling at me but avoiding Yochan's eyes. Incredibly, she went about her duties with the same cheerfulness that had endeared her to me in the first place. But on the third day, I sat her down under the over-arching beams and burnished bamboo of the ceiling. An embarrassed Yochan consented to act as interpreter.

"Suzuki-san," I began. "We are glad that you are back."

She smiled brightly, still avoiding Yochan's gaze.

"I hope we can all live together without any more crises. No one wants you to leave, certainly not Yochan. He hired you in the first place. Now he pays your salary. He brought you back three years ago because he needs and likes you."

I explained that Yochan had found and built the minka, that it was his home. Whatever happened, he would not leave.

"He may not have shown it, but he admires you greatly," I continued. "So what I am asking you should not be too difficult. I want you and Yochan, for all our sakes, to be friends."

She looked at me stonily.

"You mean I have to be friends with Yochan if I want to stay?" she asked.

I nodded.

"*De wa*, in that case, *sayonara*," she said in a voice so low I could hardly hear it, "good bye."

With that, this most unpredictable yet industrious of women, this mixture of sunshine and rain, rose to her feet, went briskly to the kitchen, wrapped her belongings and walked out of our lives.

Two weeks later, I was astonished to see Suzuki-san back in the garden. I didn't know what she had told the owner, now the farmer's widow, and didn't want to. She smiled at me in the friendliest way and exchanged a few pleasantries. From that time on we came across her plodding up the steep hill pulling a small airline baggage cart behind her in which she had packed work clothes and garden tools.

From early morning until dusk she coaxed the land to yield, as before, its rich bounty of crops.

For several years she sowed and reaped without making any overtures to Yochan or me. Then one day, she paused to talk animatedly with Katoji, in Kamakura on a visit. When they had finished, she told him to wait a moment and went into the garden where she filled a paper bag with potatoes. She gave it to him.

This created a mild sensation in the minka's kitchen.

"What does it mean?" I asked. "Is it a gesture of reconciliation? A flag of peace?"

Katoji opened the bag. Half of the potatoes were perfect, unblemished testimonials to her genius as a farmer. The rest were rotten.

Yochan

The Bamboo Curtain, which descended over China in 1949, showed no sign of lifting twenty-two years later. I was in Japan because it was an ideal place from which to follow developments—at a distance—on the communist mainland. Like all China watchers then, I bombarded Peking with requests for a visa. Silence.

The years between 1970 and 1972 produced events that intimately affected my life and Yochan's.

In April 1971, the Chinese government invited the U.S. table tennis team to visit China. They were the first Americans since 1949 to do so. After years of hostility, this was a break-through in U.S.-China relations. I was one of the only three American correspondents given a visa to cover the trip.

Yochan loaned me his camera, embraced me, and bade me godspeed. When the Chinese premier Chou En-lai said I had opened the China door, I had my fifteen minutes of fame, and expected to be among the thousand other journalists accompanying Richard Nixon to Peking the following year. I nearly quit AP when its general manager chose someone else.

"You've been," he said.

I went on a lecture tour of America instead, and returned to find Yochan's antique business humming. I got some consolation when a United Press International reporter and I were the only foreign correspondents allowed to accompany Prime Minister Tanaka to Peking that same year on a trip, which brought about diplomatic relations between China and Japan seven years before Washington could do the same.

These were my really busy years. In 1970 Yukio Mishima committed ceremonial suicide after failing to raise the Japanese army in revolt. Lin Piao, China's defense minister, whom I'd met in Manchuria years earlier, died in a plane crash after plotting to overthrow Mao.

In 1972 the United States returned Okinawa to Japan after years of tumult and anti-American demonstrations, both of which I reported. Japan surged ahead economically, piling up the first of its big trade surpluses with the United States.

The general prosperity rubbed off on the real estate market. The house and land, which had cost me a pittance, were now worth a fortune. I wasn't getting any younger and began to worry what would happen if I died without a will. By every standard I could think of, this now-valuable piece of Great Peak land belonged to Yochan and the Takishitas. I contacted a lawyer and learned a will would not be enough. In Japan, inheritance taxes are huge if property is left to someone outside the family. The lawyer suggested I adopt Yochan, making him family. In America adoption is difficult and is usually restricted to that of children. But Japan has a long history of adoption of adults, to provide an heir to a childless family.

Yochan liked the idea of formally becoming my son, of calling me *otosan*, honorable father. He said he would be happy to do so even without the property. Katoji and Kazu gave their warm approval. After years of good fortune at the hands of the Takishitas, I thought myself lucky to at last be joined to them through Yochan.

The adoption process couldn't have been simpler. I typed up a letter, which Yochan translated. It was presented to the

Kamakura city hall along with my signature and an official seal, regarded in Japan as more binding than a signature. Within an hour, the documents were drawn up. Besides the official papers, I received a kind of certificate, suitable for framing. To make sure the glue would hold, I wrote my will in English and Japanese then registered it with a Japanese notary. I also reported my action to the state of Maine and was told that adoption of adults was legal there. No other formalities were required. Yochan was twenty-seven, and I thirty years older.

Fences

According to the poet Robert Frost, good fences make good neighbors. That may be true in New England, but not Kamakura. My neighbor put up a fence, and we became enemies.

In 1976, nine years after Yochan had erected the Nomura minka, a second house rose on the Great Peak next to it. The new neighbor, let's call him Kato, was Yochan's age, friendly, and single. But he had no feeling for architecture. He threw up a drab, one-story ferro-concrete house, painted gray, which looked like an ugly duckling beside the stately magnificence of my minka.

Though we winced every time we walked past it, we could not help liking Kato-san. He worked hard, plunged enthusiastically into the activities of the water association, and didn't hesitate in the coldest weather to strip down to his underpants and dive into the chilly water of the tank to see what had gone wrong.

We didn't see each other socially, but Yochan exchanged friendly greetings with him, stopped to chat whenever he could. After a while, he married, and in time there were two well-behaved children. Yochan and I considered ourselves lucky to have such a good neighbor.

Yochan's antique business prospered from the start. Now he needed to expand; the second floor had become too small. And, though I said it didn't bother me, he worried about the stream of visitors passing through the living room to get to it. He had begun actively looking for a piece of land nearby where he could put up another minka devoted solely to his antiques.

Not long afterward, he learned the landowner north of Kato, an airline executive, was about to build. Since his lot sat back about fifteen yards from the city road on which Kato and I fronted, he would have to bring his building materials up the common path we shared. Though there was no written agreement that said so, it was understood that the path was accessible to anyone.

Yochan and I were astonished to be told one day that Kato had refused to allow his prospective neighbor use of his half of the path. This made it physically impossible for the airline man to build his house.

Even more astonishing was Kato's brazen offer, after that, to buy the land from him. Seeing through this ruse, the airline man exclaimed: "I wouldn't sell it to you if you were the last man on earth!"

Yochan had kept his distance from the quarrel until then. He now made an offer for the land, which the owner accepted. It would be ideal as Yochan's sales center. He already had a name for it: The West Gallery of the House of Antiques.

But Kato, defeated in his plan to force the airline man into selling to him, took a step that also effectively prevented Yochan from building his West Gallery on the newly purchased lot. He had thwarted the airline man merely by verbally denying him use of the path. To hinder Yochan, he took a more concrete step: he strung a flimsy rope fence down its middle. Craftily, he temporarily leased the eastern end of the overgrown field north of our minka and put up a small rope fence there, closing off all access to Yochan's plot. It was check and checkmate for Yochan. The electric crane he had brought to the peak sat idly by, immobilized by Kato's moves. It couldn't get to the site.

Puzzlement succeeded Yochan's dismay and anger. Neither he nor I could figure out Kato's motive. Was it revenge because Yochan had succeeded where he had failed? It seemed out of character. But then everything Kato had done in these past few months ran counter to the easygoing, pleasant, good-neighbor image he had so carefully cultivated.

The fence was an insubstantial thing, no more than sagging ropes and skinny posts, but it might have been the Berlin Wall at its most immovable, since neither Yochan nor I were willing to take the easy step of tearing it down. We respected our other new neighbors too much to do that. For we believed that they also were involved in a principle that applied to everyone: the free use of commonly held paths all over the Great Peak.

Hated symbol of a once-cherished neighbor turned enemy, the fence made Yochan and I acutely uncomfortable each day as we walked past it. Like a giant centipede, it created uneasiness in the entire neighborhood. Some avoided looking at it and no one got close, as if fearing it might suddenly come alive and sink its poison fangs into them.

Recalling that go-betweens are the tools of choice in Japanese disagreements, Yochan hired a lawyer to mediate. All he got was a whopping bill.

The fence created tensions among the members of the water association. Meetings were strained and uneasy. Kato, pale and tense, sat at one end of the room, Yochan and I at the other. We did not speak. Most of the members, aware they wouldn't be there if it hadn't been for Yochan and me, secretly sympathized with us. But the issue never surfaced. Instead, it festered like an open wound, destroying the unfettered happiness we had known since we stumbled upon the Great Peak.

The delay in building the West Gallery was costing Yochan dearly. The carpenters, plasterers, roofers, and other craftsmen from Shirotori were standing by. They had to be paid to wait.

Then in the spring, ten months after the start of his campaign of harassment, Kato brought in workers to add a second story to his house. Working overtime, they completed the job in a few months, then covered the house with a shiny new coat of white paint. With a touch here and there, they made it look like a Spanish villa. The ugly duckling had become a passable swan. The surprises continued. The day after the workers left, the fence came down.

This sudden end to a long dose of psychological warfare nearly put Yochan and me in shock. Throughout all this activity, Kato said nothing. Three days later, he piled his wife and children into a car and his furniture into a moving van and left. He had given up residence on the Great Peak.

It turned out he had sold the house and land to a Tokyo businesswoman, owner of a factory turning out baby clothes. Kato had told her that her land extended out to the middle of the infamous common path. He encouraged her to build a solid wall there. She did, but apologized to Yochan later when she learned of the controversy.

The landowners who had supported Kato had their comeuppance. They were able to live with the rope-and-post wall, but waxed indignant over the more solid, permanent one. They insisted the new owner open a space in it, which would allow them to walk freely up and down the controversial path. She did but it didn't last. For all practical purposes the path had shrunk to half its width. The wall had made the whole path unusable.

It took months to find out why Kato had deliberately prevented Yochan from building the West Gallery. After he lost the land to Yochan, he decided to sell his house and move. He believed the second floor and the white paint would make it more saleable. But he feared if Yochan built first, he would oppose the second story on the grounds that it blocked the sun. Japan has laws against depriving anyone from enjoying the sunshine. The courts once even ruled in favor of a plaintiff who complained he was deprived of the view of sacred Mt. Fuji.

"If Kato-san had talked to me," Yochan said ruefully, "he would have learned that the West Gallery had no windows facing south. He didn't need the fence. He could have built a ten-story building and I wouldn't have cared."

Life of the Party

Dr. Masanobu Tanaka, swarthy, fiftyish, fun-loving, and his thirty-something, blonde, talkative Danish wife were, to use a hackneyed phrase, the life of the party. They brightened the occasional small parties Yochan and I gave in the minka. But they were in their glory when they hosted parties in their own large, modern house-cum-clinic-hospital near the Inagakis. To these came Scandinavian diplomats, journalists, artists, students, and Japanese politicians. Often, because they had so many interests and so many friends, their parties were staged in a hotel or a large restaurant complex. Staged was the word; these evenings had a theme with costumes, music, and entertainment to match.

One day they invited Yochan and me to one of the biggest parties they had ever given, a night of old Hawaii, complete with leis, roast suckling pig, two-finger poi, hula shirts, and dreamy Hawaiian music. There were more than fifty guests, so it took place in a large restaurant near Kamakura.

At the end of the lavish feast, I swallowed a lump of rice as hard as a rock. The next morning I awoke with the mother of all bellyaches, unable to stand or sit without feeling a sharp pain. Yochan took me to Dr. Tanaka's, where I was diagnosed as suffering from the summer flu even though I complained the pain was in my right side, the usual symptom of appendicitis. Two days later I was still in agony and the doctor came to the minka at Yochan's request. He hadn't taken any tests on the previous occasion and didn't this time. But he saw something was seriously wrong and ordered me to the nearby Fujisawa City Hospital.

I was luckier than Yochan had been when he came down with oyster poisoning in 1967. The Fujisawa City Hospital is large and modern, staffed by nurses in crisp white uniforms and well-trained, highly skilled doctors. I was their first foreign patient.

The chief surgeon Dr. Chitake Kasaoka put me through the usual tests.

"You have a ruptured appendix and peritonitis has set in," he said through Yochan. "We will have to operate at once."

Within an hour I was on the operating table under a spinal anesthetic, conscious of everything that went on. Thanks to a tranquilizer I was cheerful as a cricket throughout the proceedings. But Yochan, told how low my white blood cells had sunk, gloomily reflected, as the gurney was wheeled into the operating room, that this could be the last time he saw me alive.

Dr. Kasaoka, middle-aged, affable, and able to speak understandable English, explained that if he had not removed the poison sloshing around in my belly, I would have died.

"Twenty years ago," he added, "nothing would have helped. Death was inevitable."

A year later, I retired from the AP and spent several months traveling Europe. When I came back, Yochan told me a tale about the Tanakas that sounded like a Greek tragedy.

His vivacious wife, so full of life and laughter, came down with breast cancer. The doctor, anguished, abandoned his practice to be with her. But within six months she was dead. Sorrowfully he laid her ashes to rest in her native Copenhagen.

Within months he too was dead, some say by his own hand, others of a broken heart.

Yochan and Reiko are wed, 1983.

After all these tragedies, there was a bright note. Yochan married Reiko, his secretary of several years, and began a new and exciting period in his life.

In 1985, the Foreign Correspondents' Club of Japan celebrated its fortieth anniversary with a gala black-tie dinner in a Tokyo hotel. I was asked, as a former president, to be the master of ceremonies. The honored guests were Crown Prince Akihito and his wife, later to become the emperor and empress of Japan.

Dismayed to find my formal, black-tie dress suit riddled with moth holes, I borrowed Yochan's formal Japanese ceremonial garb, called a *hakama*. In this traditional black silk costume, elaborately belted and wearing a ceremonial flower, I stood in elegant contrast to the 500 other guests, all in drab Western tuxedos.

I explained to applause that I had chosen it to honor the Club's Japanese members, a sentiment that evoked warm applause from the imperial couple. It drew an even warmer reaction from the conservative, tradition-minded prime minister, Yasuhiro Nakasone, who dropped by before the event to extend his best wishes.

Several months later, obviously impressed, he nominated me to receive the Order of the Sacred Treasure, with neck ribbon.

Yochan joined me at a reception in the foreign ministry and drove me to the palace in the center of Tokyo. There Akihito's father, the late Emperor Hirohito, presided gravely over the solemn ceremonies for the thousand other honorees. I was the only American.

As I left, spangled order of the decoration around my neck, I reflected that for a young reporter who had hated Japan in 1941, I had come full circle.

They meet Crown Prince Akihito and the crown princess at the press club's fortieth anniversary party.

Dressed in Yochan's wedding hakama, I win the admiration of a prime minister.

Minkas Domestic

The West Gallery, which Yochan hastened to build as soon as the Kato fence came down, was his third minka.

"Never again," he said wearily, when he finished my minka in 1967. "I never want to build another minka. It's too exhausting."

But a year before the Kato fence episode, he received two visitors to his second-floor gallery who changed all that. They were Ernie Salomon, an American businessman in Tokyo, and his Japanese wife Yae.

They came to look at Yochan's collection of antiques, which was becoming known in the Tokyo area, and, indeed, as far off as the United States and Europe. His early clients told their friends and they passed on the word to others. He hadn't spent a single yen on advertising. It was all word of mouth.

After three years of satisfying growth, Yochan was sure he had made the right choice in becoming a dealer. It brought him into intimate touch with the Japanese art scene. Besides foreigners from many nations, he received some of the more knowledgeable Japanese collectors. Now thirty, fluent in English, and at ease with visitors from many social and economic levels, he was a far cry from the youth who had hitchhiked around the world.

It was the Salomons' first visit to the minka and its upstairs gallery. Taking off their shoes in the genkan, they stepped up into the high-ceilinged living room and looked with wonder at the web of highly polished pillars and beams. It was a bright day and the sun shone through the glass windows, highlighting the azaleas, camellias, and pines outside.

Yae gasped. "Ernie," she blurted out, "get me one of these for my birthday!"

An exemplary husband, he did.

That was how Yochan added the rescue and renovation of old farmhouses to his prospering antique business.

Prodded by Yae and encouraged by Ernie, he found an old farmhouse in the Gifu mountains and had it dismantled and shipped by truck to Karuizawa, a popular mountain resort north of Tokyo. Already the owner of other houses, Ernie wanted the minka as a country villa.

His land, on a gently sloping hill, lay on the outskirts of Karuizawa. There were no neighbors to complicate the process. Water, pumped in from the city, was abundant and cheap. The difficulty was access. The dirt road leading to the site was muddy. Trucks and cranes got bogged down and had to be pulled out. Yochan built a solid road, and work began.

Ernie's villa, with its steep snow roof, was highly visible, perched on his hill. Yochan installed not only an irori, a floor fireplace, but also a western-style fireplace in the living room. Ernie also insisted on an oil-burning space heater, which could be started by telephone from Tokyo. The Karuizawa winters are numbingly cold. Unlike Meredith Weatherby, Ernie was ready to pay anything to keep warm.

Yochan built a wide porch all around the house so they could enjoy the mountain scenery. From the second floor, they had a stunning view of Mt. Asama, an extinct volcano, which looks very much like Mt. Fuji.

Yochan's West Gallery confronted him with a challenge different from that of my minka or Ernie Salomon's. One was a permanent residence, the other a vacation home. The West Gallery would be a showcase for Yochan's growing collection of Japanese and Chinese art and antiques. It would serve as a guest house, hold parties, and was even a residence for a while. But its primary purpose was as a sales center.

With it, Yochan struck out on his own. The House of Antiques would no longer grace my second floor. He had earned enough from his antique sales and the Salomon minka to be totally independent.

Until this point he had not taken advantage of the ideas gained from a study of Meredith Weatherby's minka in Tokyo, but they figured prominently in the West Gallery, beginning with an entranceway of brick rather than pounded earth.

Weatherby's architect had taken a plain, ordinary minka and jazzed it up to make it more attractive and livable. Yochan rationalized the liberties he was about to take: this minka was for commercial rather than residential use. He was careful, however, to preserve its integrity by making sure the changes or additions followed the intention, if not the letter, of the original. He put in a western-style foundation as he had with my minka and Ernie Salomon's. And once again he flouted feng shui, making the whole structure face east rather than south. He kept the roof as steep as it had been in the country, but instead of black slate, chose a yellowish tar-based composition shingle.

"It's cheaper," he said, "but it also looks more like thatch than the slate."

He meticulously reassembled the primary and secondary beams and pillars exactly as they had been. This was an architectural necessity. To have done otherwise would have invited possible collapse of the entire structure.

The major innovations Yochan gleaned from Weatherby's example were made in the interior and consisted of double tokonoma and numerous recesses for displaying screens, scrolls, and other art objects. Because he preferred warmth over authenticity, Yochan installed in the living-room floor copper pipes the thickness of a finger through which hot water circulated, warming the room as the Koreans do. Regular hot-water radiators supplemented this floor-heating system. Because the heat would warp the original wide, old boards of the house, he substituted straw matting. The addition of a Tudor-style fireplace made the room the warmest, perhaps, in Kamakura. For the next fourteen years while we shivered in the old minka—I still couldn't afford central heating—Yochan and I escaped to the West Gallery to keep warm in winter.

Since it had no windows on the south, Yochan turned the north wall into glass, as he had done with my minka. But he covered the windows in paper sliding doors called *shoji*, which he could close to create the mood of a genuine Japanese country house. Besides, he wanted his customers to look in, where the for-sale masterpieces were, rather than out.

Despite the ingenious alterations—they included a central vacuum cleaning system that had ports on all three floors into which one could plug the cleaner head—the most dramatic aspect of the first floor was its ceiling of new bamboo and its network of four massive beams held together by a long, curved central beam. One of the transverse beams rested over this keystone beam, the second under, the third over, and the last under. It was as though the original daiku-san sought, in this extraordinary way, to give the impression of weaving. What he produced was a wooden sculpture any museum would covet. It made a statement as powerful as the minka itself.

Mounting steep stairs to the next floor revealed another example of Yochan's ingenuity. There is a dead space between the first and second floors in most minkas set aside for storage. In the gallery it was a low, windowless area usable for little else. Yochan raised its ceiling to make it possible to walk upright. He cut out windows that brought in light and air, laid a tatami floor, and built recesses for his porcelains. Chinese furniture, rich oriental carpets, and screens made this formerly useless space a much-remarked-upon mezzanine floor. Small teahouse doors at its entrance forced the visitor to stoop to get in, an intended exercise in humility consonant with the dignity of the tea ceremony.

Yochan also opened interior windows from this reclaimed room, which looked down on the fireplace in the room below. At night its wood fires threw dancing lights on the reed-covered ceiling. On festive occasions, with many guests present, these windows provided vantage points from which one could hear and see a string quartet playing Vivaldi on the first floor.

Yochan turned the third floor into a study containing his art books. A large window looked west toward Mt. Fuji, visible on a rare clear day.

"It's a Hiroshige!" I would exclaim, confusing art with nature, as the great orb of the sun painted the sky with layers of red in its slow descent behind the sacred mountain.

Above the bookcases Yochan built a tatami-covered loft, an ideal sleeping space for the young and young at heart. There were no protective rails to prevent sleepwalkers from falling into the study below.

The sloping third-floor ceiling of the new West Gallery turned out to be a triumph of Yochan's imagination. He forced wet plaster between narrow strips of reeds as he had done with the split bamboo of the small roof in my minka. The alternating white of the plaster and the brown of the reeds created a texture of great warmth and beauty.

In a final irony of the fence incident, the West Gallery was joined to what was once the Kato residence. Because the new owner came infrequently, she readily consented to rent her ground floor to Yochan to use as his architectural design center. With her approval, he built a roofed area between the two houses for storage and protection against the elements. A successful businesswoman, she was superstitious and insisted that the rent Yochan pay her contain the number eight, a good-luck number.

Despite much prodding, he refused to disclose to me whether the number appeared first or last.

Yae Salomon didn't realize it, but she set in motion a twin career for Yochan, as a builder, which rivals and sometimes exceeds that of antique collector.

Up to the time of this writing, he has taken down, moved, and put up over thirty minkas, almost all in Japan.

One went to Buenos Aires and three, knocked together as one, have risen in an exclusive part of Honolulu. In addition, he has designed and built a large, graceful guesthouse for a Shinto shrine near Tokyo, which is his masterpiece.

If all these minkas were the same, it would be tiresome to describe them. But a few are so different, and the stories surrounding their resurrection so unusual, they are worth describing.

Rokuro Omura was a justly famed Japanese artist whose paintings are vivid, semi-abstract, and almost brutal in their subjects and coloring. So when he commissioned a minka from Yochan, both he and I wondered whether he would settle for the conservative tastes of the countryside. It soon became apparent he had no intention of doing so.

Though he does not insist upon it, most Japanese and foreign clients accept Yochan's ideas, worked out after consultation, for the restoration of the old folk houses they have bought. After all, he is the expert, and they generally know little or nothing about them.

Yochan hesitated when Omura-sensei (artists, doctors, professors and other such professionals are called *sensei*, or master, rather than the merely honorific *san*) told him what he wanted to do. But since he had immense respect for his genius and accepted the fact that artists are not conformists, he agreed.

The result shocked me. I admired Picasso, Dali, Hieronymus Bosch, and the innovative architecture of Arthur Erickson, but liked my minkas straight.

Omura-sensei quite clearly imposed his strong personality on his minka.

Seen from the outside, it has the distinctive lines of the real thing. But at Omura's command, its walls are neither wood nor tin, but plaster painted a rusty red, like those of Beijing's Forbidden City. The genkan is flanked by a large glass hothouse filled with plants. Nothing wrong there, but it is hardly traditional.

The living room is imposing, as it is in all minkas, with its large posts and beams, but its walls also are red. French chandeliers hang incongruously from the ceiling. Heavy plush curtains frame the pristine white of the sliding shoji. A narrow iron balcony, like those in large libraries, runs along one wall, but there are no books to take down and read.

A fire-engine red spiral staircase at one end of this highly eclectic room leads to the second floor. It, at least, is wide and easily managed. Bedrooms, a sauna, toilet, and a kitchen, none terribly radical, occupy this floor.

The third floor is a major surprise. In a minka, the steepness of the roof militates against a third floor at all. But Yochan met Omura-sensei's desire for a sunlit studio by changing the roof's angle. The darkness of the original minka now is replaced by the sun pouring into a tall room with floor-to-ceiling windows, rather like French doors. This willingness to alter the roof to meet a special need is yet another example of Yochan's flexibility and originality. Paintings on easels and hanging from hooks lend an air of excitement to this room, which has been created out of nothing.

Omura-sensei's atelier reveals a man of vivid imagination and powerful emotions, not at all what I expected of the slender, almost emaciated man I met through Yochan. Secretly I wished I could afford to buy one of his paintings.

There is a large unfurnished fourth floor reached by a ladder made of crosswise strips of wood nailed to a steep riser. Omura-sensei scrambled up it like a boy, but I tried it and gave up.

Like a fisherman, Yochan can tell you about the minkas that got away. But he doesn't enjoy doing so because people, not fish, were involved.

One of them was a French winemaker settled in California. He wanted a guesthouse for his very modern winery. His

Japanese wife suggested a minka. A Tokyo real estate company recommended Yochan and they duly visited my house on the Great Peak, expressing pleasure in what they saw. Yochan was delighted. When they discussed which architect to use, Yochan proposed the award-winning Canadian Arthur Erickson, an old friend. The project interested him. The vintner counter-proposed an equally famous architect. Then there was silence.

Much later, the winemaker wrote to ask Yochan if he would like to buy a disassembled minka lying on his property. He had gone to Gifu, found a minka, had it moved, and then ran into a wall. He couldn't find anyone able to put it up.

Even more disappointing was the behavior of a famous Japanese movie actress and her American-educated businessman husband. They read about Yochan and came to the Great Peak to talk about building a minka. Repeated visits resulted in intimacy. Both Yochan and I were charmed by her graciousness and impressed by his wit and English fluency. Yochan drew up forty blueprints and the project seemed well under way.

Remembering my unfavorable reactions to the Nomura minka when I saw it in its unvarnished state, Yochan made it a rule not to show minkas to prospective clients. They had to trust him.

The beautiful actress and her husband apparently did not. They sweet-talked him into making a trip to Gifu to help them find their dream minka. A week later, he learned they had gone over his head and secretly attempted to buy it themselves.

Yochan's reaction was one of pain rather than anger. On my advice, he wrote that he was disappointed in them, and had expected more from such superior people. Stung, they sent him a check for the blueprints in the next mail, and then built the minka themselves.

Leafing through a glossy Japanese magazine one day, Yochan came across an interview with the actress in which she revealed how she had stumbled across this lovely old minka during one of her rambles in the countryside. There was no mention of Yochan.

Though he no longer owned it, Yochan felt a pang of sadness when one of his old minkas, sold to a well-known sculptor in Shikoku, went up in flames. To get it to this smallest of the Japanese main islands, he had to move the heavy timbers by car ferry. The bridge that now links it and Honshu had not yet been built.

The setting, in the midst of a colony of sculptors—Isamu Noguchi and Masayuki Nagare were neighbors—was grand. The owner, a purist in love with old folk houses, left it exactly as Yochan had rebuilt it. No frills, no fancy additions. No western furniture. It was stunning in its unadorned beauty.

But he made a bad mistake. He decided to use it as a workshop. One day, his young son, himself a sculptor, applied the searing heat of a gas jet to metal. The gas cylinder exploded, severely burning him. Within minutes the lovely old building had burned to the ground.

My minka nearly suffered the same fate. Alfred Hitchcock, in true suspense fashion, came to the rescue.

Yochan and I decided one summer night to stay home and watch a Hitchcock thriller, *The Birds*, on television, rather than go out for dinner as planned. When we were half through it, in the kitchen, Yochan heard a noise in the living room. Opening the door, we saw flames leaping up from the hot-air furnace below the stairs. In the spring, when heating was no longer necessary, I had thrown a scatter rug over the furnace grate to conceal it. Someone had brushed against the thermostat on an adjoining pillar, and two months later the heat reached the critical point, igniting the rug.

Yochan picked it up, still burning, and threw it out the window, then smothered the flames around the furnace with a fire extinguisher. I got up at three o'clock the next morning to find it burning again and doused it with water.

Had we gone out to dinner that night, we would have returned to a pile of charred wood.

The hot-air furnace was one of my unsuccessful efforts to keep the minka warm during the fourteen years before I could afford central heating. It delivered a powerful blast of heat, which went straight up to the high ceiling and stayed there. Attempts to drive it down with electric fans failed miserably.

I thought I had found the solution with three large triangular heaters burning propane gas. They couldn't make a dent in the mass of arctic air hovering in the enormous room. They were a dismal failure on the very first New Year's Eve I celebrated in the minka. Jean Pearce, a *Japan Times* columnist; Bob Poos, the AP's Tokyo news editor, and his wife; and Sam Jones, the AP's photo chief were there. Yochan was traveling. The cold was bone chilling. So much so that the wooden typhoon shutters, *amado*, were closed tight. As the bells of Kamakura's temples tolled the end of the year, the frozen inmates opened the shutters a crack to hear them, and then quickly shut them again. The only thing that saved them was a large pot of chili con carne brought by the Poos. Everyone slept that morning fully dressed under blankets.

Not long after that, I got a fright when the kerosene boiler in the kitchen, used to supply hot water, exploded with a roar like that of a jet engine and turned a fiery red. I shut it off and ordered a new electric one the next day.

Gardens, Stones, and Buddhas

When I bought the Great Peak land in 1967 I felt confident it would be big enough not only for the Nomura minka, but a large garden as well. It wasn't. Instead I got three small gardens on the south, east, and west. There was space enough on the north for a path leading to the entranceway. The large piece of land, which Kato had leased in the "war of the fences," was overrun with weeds, tall grass, bushes, and trees. It lay there unused for years while I dreamt of one day being able to buy it. These dreams slowly dissipated into thin air as land prices escalated out of reach and the owner showed no signs of selling.

I consoled myself with the thought that we had a garden that was matchless, something the Japanese call a *shakkei*, or borrowed view, on the south. It was an endless and ever-changing panorama of the distant woods, town, and ocean.

At about this time, an impressive collection of Buddhist statuary, votary stones, wooden *Kannon* statues, and stone lanterns came on the market. Yochan bought the lot and had them desanctified twice by a priest. That turned them from religious icons into simple art objects.

The question then arose: where could they be placed? He put some of them in my three small gardens, but after that there were many left over. He took a chance, without contacting the landowners, and positioned a dozen of them on the sloping ground north of the West Gallery and the rest along the narrow path north of my minka.

Since the West Gallery's completion, Yochan had tried in vain to reach the owner of the fifty tsubo of land north of it. Telephone calls, letters, telegrams, and enquiries at the city office yielded no information. No one seemed to know where he was. On the assumption, already proven in the building of my minka, that nothing goes unnoticed in Japan, Yochan suspected that with the appearance of the stones he would be hearing from him. Sure enough, two days later, a representative of the landlord knocked on his door and politely inquired if Yochan was interested in the land. He said he was. The next day the landlord, living in Osaka eight hours away by train, arrived. Over a bowl of *soba* noodles, they agreed to the sale and the stones had a permanent home.

His new land was vacant except for the figures. Within a week, thanks to the genius of Japanese gardeners, it was a luxurious grove of tall bamboo trees swaying in the breeze. The gardeners brought them in trucks and planted them in the ground in what seemed no time at all.

I worried about the stones standing on my neighbor's land. I thought, like Yochan, the owner would appear and something could be arranged. But he didn't. He lived in Chiba prefecture, five hours from Kamakura, and presumably had no friends to tip him off.

I consulted Noguchi-san, our best friend among our neighbors. One of the original owners, he was a Great Peak elder, highly respected and often asked for advice. Both he and his wife were unfailingly generous to both of us.

Noguchi-san agreed to serve as go-between and contact the owner. I asked him to offer him 129,000 yen a tsubo for a strip two meters wide running from west to east. I figured that would be sufficient to accommodate the stones already there. Since this was about a third of the going price for land at that time, I had little hope it would be accepted.

Noguchi came back with an unexpected counter-proposal: buy the entire 200-tsubo field for 70,000 yen a tsubo. Hastily checking my resources I found I had $50,000 in Citibank certificates of deposit, the exact amount; the lecture tour and careful savings had improved my bank balance. It would wipe me out financially, just as the minka had, but I believed it a chance too good to miss. I dreamt of having a large garden almost more than I had wanted a house.

"It's a deal," I told Noguchi.

Two days later I went to Tokyo with Yochan and exchanged a check for the land deed. The garden seemed on the verge of realization.

The next day the alarm bells went off at the bank, next door to the headquarters of AP at 50 Rockefeller Plaza, New York City. I had telegraphed the bank to transfer all my CDs to my checking account, confident that I had notified it in time to cover the check. In banking matters, as in other things, I was just the slightest bit naïve.

"You cannot cash your CDs before their term is up," the bank wired sternly. "There will be no transfer to the checking account until then."

That meant waiting four more months.

I always paid my bills promptly and owed no one. I didn't believe in borrowing. I had for more than twenty years been the very image of fiscal probity. I realized with a start that I had just passed a $50,000 bad check, a crime punishable, I supposed, with imprisonment on bread and water, perhaps fiendish torture as well.

In my hour of need, I turned to old Mother AP.

"Can't you do something about this?" I asked the treasurer by phone. "I've banked with these people for twenty years. All AP's accounts are with Citibank. Can't they bend the rules a bit?"

They could, but reluctantly. It would cash the CDs and transfer the amount to the checking account. But I would lose $1,200 in interest as a penalty. Relieved, I sighed and accepted my punishment. The Japanese bank happily cleared the check by mail. By the time it reached New York, it was no longer rubber, but as good as gold.

Months later I learned why I had been sold the land for so generous a price. It was classified as non-residential and no building could be erected on it. To most people it would have been regarded as almost worthless and the price exorbitant. But since I wanted it solely as a garden and had no intention of building on it, I was completely satisfied.

The dollar-to-yen exchange rate was on a roller coaster those days. Had I waited six months, the dollar equivalent for the garden would have been $100,000. I would not have been able to buy it.

Our garden evolved in three stages. Yochan commissioned an award-winning father-and-son gardening team to clear the land and chop down several old and ugly trees, letting in the sunlight. They spared two large cherry trees and a smaller maple and planted tall corals, which formed a 20-foot wall of green on the north. Magnolia, plum, pine, peach, apple, small maple, orange, and persimmon trees followed.

In leveling the ground preparatory to building my minka in 1967 the bulldozer driver had ignored orders to spare the lone surviving tree. He cut it off at its base. Its loss pained us. In an act of atonement, we planted dozens of trees in the new garden. Years

later, to our astonishment, a sturdy tree grew out of the stump
of the decapitated one.

Yochan rescued the assorted stone lanterns, pagodas, votive
statues, and stone Buddhas from their cramped space along the
north path and distributed them decoratively in the new garden.
If they could have spoken, they undoubtedly would have thanked
him for letting them breathe more freely in a setting more suitable
to their once-exalted place in life.

Knowing my fondness for the small garden on the west
where I used to spend quiet moments lost in reverie, Yochan
embellished it with a Japanese *toro* lantern and a ten-foot-tall
Chinese column on whose top squatted a pudgy stone lion.
He placed the other column in front of the West Gallery to
symbolize its tie to my minka.

Four extraordinary stone figures flanked the east side of
the path leading to the entranceway. Their origins were obscure.
Yochan thought they dated from the sixteenth century and may
have been associated with the arrival of the Portuguese. About
three feet high, they resembled Christian crusaders dressed in
headdresses of mail. Two wielded staffs or pikes, which struck
at dragons groveling at their feet.

Many of the stones in the garden bore inscriptions in
Japanese. Intrigued, I asked Reiko the meaning of a single
character on one of them.

"It is *mu*," she said, "the character for nothingness.
It is part of a Zen riddle, or *koan*."

Impressed, I pointed to a stone lantern that bore
many characters. Surely it would be even more mystifying.

"It says," said Reiko, "*Stone lantern*."

Since the surface of the new garden was nearly two feet higher than the genkan entranceway, it was reached by a wooden ramp. I thought of it as a hanging garden. A year later, while I was traveling, Yochan turned it into a sunken garden by the simple expedient of digging floor-level paths north, west, and east. In the first phase, one got the impression of walking above everything. In the second, the garden looked down on the stroller. In the third and final stage, tons of dirt removed from the foundation of the new garage and annex were turned into a gentle hill, which gave the garden a new character.

My sole contribution, besides advice seldom heeded, was a blanket of varicolored African pansies just outside the kitchen window. Durable flowers, they survived sixteen snowfalls one winter and came up jauntier than ever each time.

In its final version, the garden defies classification. It is neither French nor English, and too undisciplined to be called Japanese. One's eyes are drawn, as one enters through the striking wooden gate Yochan gave me for my seventy-fifth birthday, to a raised area on the north, festooned with small votive stones. It is a Buddhist chorus in full chant.

The sunken paths are floored with stone slabs. Small, ridged millstones beckon one toward the weathered wooden doors of the genkan. A stone bench sits under one of the maples and the pansies have long since been replaced by a carpet of green moss.

Leaving, the wooden gate is worth looking at more closely. Two Korean stone statues flank it on either side. Bought in Shikoku, the gate illustrates the Japanese love of imbalance, or asymmetry. It has a copper roof, an opening of wooden slats on the north, and a decorative window on the south. Its graceful lack of balance reflects the pleasing disorder inside.

Minkas Foreign

Two Argentineans in early middle age, a translator of technical manuals and his quick, intelligent wife, were frequent visitors to the Great Peak minka. Thanks to her work in a bank and his additional job with an Argentinean shipping company, they lived comfortably with a house in Hayama, near Kamakura, and an apartment in Tokyo. Neither rich nor poor, they shared Yochan's passion for old minkas and dreamt of erecting the bare bones of one outside Buenos Aires. Over the years, as their finances improved, they planned to add a roof, walls, and floor. On retirement they would not only live in it, but make it a museum to house their growing collection of Japanese folk art.

Was Yochan interested? The financial gains would be small, but he wouldn't have to worry about shipping it. The Argentinean's company would do so, for nothing.

In 1983, Yochan had married Reiko, his long-time secretary. It was a union of opposites: he is descended from a long line of sturdy rice farmers, country people; she from distinguished doctors, samurai, high court judges, an advisor to the emperor. But the ties that bind them are many. They know and admire Japanese art and culture. Each speaks fluent English (she also knows German), have traveled widely, are interested in history and foreign affairs, like classical music (she plays the ancient *koto*), enjoy good wine, and are superb cooks. It is no secret I am the chief beneficiary of all this. Thanks to them, my old age had taken on an added glow.

Because he loved old minkas and yearned one day to have a museum of his own, Yochan was not only interested but enthusiastic. He and Reiko had had a busy year and were exhausted. This was a chance for a second honeymoon in a country they had heard much about, but had never visited.

This minka, like mine, was a gassho zukuri with a steep snow roof, but one of immense size, four times as big. Owned by the descendant of twenty-nine generations of rice farmers in Fukui prefecture, it once housed as many as thirty or forty families. Shirakawa, not far from Shirotori, has houses of similar size but different style. It also resembled mine in that it was a Heike house, built by the descendants of that ill-fated twelfth-century military clan.

Despite its great size, it was graceful: its window system formed patterns that from the outside resembled a Mondrian painting. It was the granddaddy of all Yochan's minkas.

Yochan oversaw its dismantling and its movement to the port of Nagoya where the large timbers were lowered into the hold of a Buenos Aires–bound ship.

Reiko and Yochan said goodbye to me and flew from Tokyo to Argentina by way of Vancouver, taking with them two hesitant Shirotori carpenters. They were on board under duress and agreed to go only after weeks of talk with their families and friends, who regarded venturing so far from Shirotori as, if not dangerous, at the very least daunting. One of the imagined perils was the long air flight: neither had flown before nor ventured farther afield than Nagoya. Would they be able to get the fermented beans and rice they were used to? It was highly problematical. When they left, they were given a sendoff more gloomy than glad.

Airborne, given a choice, they had fish rather than steak, which they neither knew nor liked. They learned, with a measure of unease, that Argentina was famous for its beef and probably had nothing else. They rejected the proffered bread and took rice.

The six Argentinean carpenters working with them spoke only Spanish. But through signs, gestures, smiles, frowns, and other body language, they got on famously. When things became too technical, the owners stepped in.

And the Japanese carpenters soon got over their aversion to beef.

"We had it three times a day, better than anything I have ever eaten," said Yochan. "In Japan each meal would have cost fifty dollars. We paid fifty cents."

Assembling the skeleton, large as it was, took only thirty days. Yochan and Reiko look back on this adventure in Argentina as one of the pleasantest in their lives. It was 1984, the year of my retirement from AP, which they helped celebrate.

"We often thought back to those carefree days," Yochan said. "There was no comparison," added Reiko.

From Japan, and during their home leaves, the young Argentineans slowly completed the huge structure that Yochan and Reiko had begun. It now is half museum, half residence. Retired, they live happily in it, surrounded by the folk craft pieces they so lovingly collected during their life in Japan.

Yochan had been collecting antiques for fourteen years when he was invited to the first Asian Antique Dealers and Collectors Conference in San Francisco. He was the only Asian. Over the years, his taste in Japanese and Chinese art had become more refined, more selective. The highly regarded Hilton Hotel chain featured his screens, some 300 years old, in two of its art magazine issues. Screens were the centerpieces of his exhibit at the conference.

Dr. Kent "Rusty" London bought one of them.

Slim, personable, young—he was Yochan's age—he had embarked on one career, given it up, and made a fortune in another. When he met Yochan, he was beginning a third. Rusty was his nickname, but he made it legal. That was typical of the boldness, audacity, and contempt for convention of this unusual American.

He spent the early years of his life studying to be a doctor, but never practiced. Gifted with total recall—he could read a book and remember all of it—he put it to work at the gaming tables of America and Europe. Able to foresee the turn of the cards in *vingt-et-un*, blackjack, he broke the bank at one casino after another. He was a millionaire before he was thirty and wrote two books recounting his adventures. Barred from the casinos—he had done nothing illegal, but this was their privilege—he took up business consulting, another gamble, some would say. One of his clients was a small machine-tool company based in New York called Wedtech.

After the conference Rusty came to Kamakura, met me, and was seduced by the minka. He returned several times after that with a proposition for Yochan: "Build a minka for me in Honolulu."

Though his home and business were in San Francisco, he had a million-dollar waterfront home in Honolulu and had just acquired a large lot almost next door. He proposed to move both home and business to Hawaii, under the capacious roof of one of Yochan's minkas.

Yochan hesitated. Constructing the Argentinean minka had been a lark. It only involved putting up the primary and secondary structures. Rusty wanted not only a minka, but a complex, including swimming pool, guesthouse, garage, teahouse, and Japanese garden.

In the end, Rusty's enthusiasm persuaded him.

Planning took months, loading the telephone circuits between Kamakura and San Francisco. Yochan decided he needed three minkas, joined as one, rather than one small minka. Fitting them together would be a challenge.

Recruiting carpenters and other craftsmen from Shirotori proved easier than in the Argentinean project. Nearly everyone in Japan knows Hawaii. Millions go there each year on holiday or on their honeymoons. It is a Pacific paradise many Japanese want to visit. The two originally reluctant carpenters of the Buenos Aires job were among the seventeen Yochan signed on. They had become instant celebrities in Shirotori on their return.

It took more than a year to tailor the pillars and beams of the three minkas in Yochan's storage site in Shirotori. Taken down in their different locations, they were trucked to Shirotori, where their all-important ends were manicured with as much care as fingernails in a beauty salon. Then Yochan, a perfectionist, did what he always did: erected the skeletons of all three to determine how they fitted and what changes or additions would be needed. That alone was an exhausting process, but it was better than finding something wrong with the structure after he got to Honolulu.

Once the inspections and adjustments had been made, the five thousand big and little pieces of these three country homes were loaded into twenty two-ton containers, trucked to the port of Nagoya eighty miles away, and put aboard a container ship bound for Honolulu.

Flying in ahead of it, Yochan had the thorny task of clearing this jumble of ancient wood through customs and getting work visas for the waiting craftsmen. He satisfied requirements that the wood be insect free—their age and the smoky wood fires of centuries took care of that. The American embassy in Tokyo, recognizing the cultural value of this Japanese transplant, lent a hand on the visas.

This was Yochan's most ambitious undertaking. The obstacles were formidable even after the men and timbers had been allowed into Honolulu. None of them spoke a word of English. Yochan, and later Reiko, had to almost literally take them by the hand when they wished to move about town. And they had to be fed. Not just any food: that of the Gifu mountains.

It already had been decided that Kazu and Katoji, eager for a Hawaiian holiday, would oversee the care and feeding of the craftsmen. Kazu had cooked when the Kamakura minka was built and felt confident she could handle this new test of her culinary skills.

One night, driving home to Shirotori from Gifu City, Katoji fell asleep at the wheel. The car smashed into a stone wall. Their knees and arms were broken. Only the fact they wore their seat belts saved them from death.

An ambulance just happened to be behind them. That saved their lives.

"You also saved us," said Kazu to me. "You nagged us for years to fasten our seat belts when we didn't want to. We had them on when we hit the wall."

The accident put both of them in the hospital for three months. Reiko replaced them.

Frail and petite, she weighs not much more than a hundred pounds, dripping wet. Though she is a city girl, she is the equal of any country woman when it comes to hard, grinding work. She could have begged off, asked Yochan to hire someone to do the cooking. But that was not in her proud nature. Her ancestors had advised emperors. What the Takishitas could do, she could do.

Reiko was not entirely comfortable in Honolulu. She had enjoyed her years in Hamburg with her first husband, a senior trade executive, but found the socially prominent Americans she met after they moved to Chicago unfeeling and unfriendly. When she organized a lunch for wives of her husband's associates, only one showed up. She recalled other instances of anti-Japanese behavior, such as when her small son Nori came home in tears one day after being jeered by his American classmates.

"Mommy," he asked, "what's Pearl Harbor?"

That Americans could be hard and cruel, even I, an American, could testify to. In 1970 I did an anniversary piece on Hiroshima—the first city ever to be atom bombed—which compared it to an elegant lady in a soiled kimono. Along with the praise, I got hate mail from Americans. Some faulted me for not mentioning Pearl Harbor, the Japanese attack that brought the United States into World War II.

"You and your type should be given a free ticket to Russia to learn the real value of liberty," wrote one from Florida. "You are a pious S.O.B. who doesn't, or does, realize the disservice he is doing a great country. You punk."

A local priest in an aloha shirt performed the ceremonies appeasing the spirits of the land on which the three-in-one minka would rise. Rusty, his new Chinese-American wife Jada, the interior designer Mark Miyasato, Yochan, Reiko, and I were there. The land, on Portlock Road, one of the best parts of town, looked out on the bay and Diamond Head in the distance.

Then the problems began for Reiko.

Rusty's large house, two doors away, was one of them. He and Jada moved into an apartment and turned it over to the visiting craftsmen. They bedded down on futons scattered around the interior.

That year was the hottest Honolulu had seen in a long time. The sun blazed with scorching intensity, unrelieved by cooling trade winds. Rusty's house had no air-conditioning.

The heat proved particularly punishing for Reiko. She tolerated it badly. In Japan she had spent ten days in a hospital after suffering from heat prostration. The kitchen was as hot as the boiler room in a slave ship. Flies, mosquitoes, and cockroaches added to the misery. No matter what she did, and that included generous potions of anti-bug poison, they flourished.

Yochan plotted to give her a rest by taking the crew to the nearest McDonald's; they refused to go again. She continued to feed them rice, noodles, bean paste soup, beef, curry, raw and cooked fish, seaweed, mountain potatoes, and oceans of green tea.

In Reiko, Yochan and the team from Shirotori got more than a cook. She also was an interpreter, liaison-chief, den mother, and gofer. The craftsmen poured their troubles into her ears. Without her there would have been chaos. Kazu and Katoji showed up halfway through the project but were too weak to help out.

Despite the deadening heat, the hard work and long hours, it was a cheerful, upbeat work crew. Both Yochan and Mark Miyasato did some of the heavy carrying, their bare skins glistening with sweat as they lugged boxes of tiles from the truck to the house. There for a month, I did little more than offer encouragement.

Yochan met each group of workers as they arrived from Japan, gave escorted tours of the Polynesian Village on the North Shore, and occasionally invited everyone to a Japanese restaurant nearby where the owner spoke the Osaka dialect with which they were familiar.

Miraculously, there were almost no accidents. One man fell off the roof and had to be hospitalized but soon recovered. Loneliness was a problem. Workers with wives either returned for brief holidays or met them in Honolulu, at Yochan's expense.

Rusty's architect and general contractor had little to do. Yochan had been architect, contractor, and general factotum for all his previous houses and found it difficult not to do the same in Honolulu. The architect, a talented Japanese-American, was fascinated by the minka style.

In its finished form, the complex included an Olympic-sized swimming pool, a garage disguised as a *kura*, or rural storage house, a teahouse, and a garage/guest apartment. A famous gardener turned the barren ground into a landscape of rocks, water, stone bridges, and sand: a bit of Japan among the waving palms.

The enlarged minka, with its network of heavy beams and pillars, fitted into the Hawaii landscape as comfortably as it had in the heavy snows of central Japan. That it did so was a tribute, again, to Yochan's genius. As he had in my minka, he opened up one long wall to the sea, letting in the abundant sunlight and air. Then he built wide verandas, what the Hawaiians call *lanais*, to open it up even further to the gardens and the bay.

A large living room containing a fireplace for the occasional chilly nights of Honolulu, a spacious straw-matted dining area raised above ground level, and a long, high-ceilinged room facing the interior garden, which would serve as Rusty's office, were the main rooms of the first floor. A modern well-equipped kitchen and toilet facilities completed the design.

Generous-sized bedrooms, baths, and lofts made up part of the second floor. To them, Rusty added a space no Japanese minka had ever known: a soundproofed, acoustically perfect chamber equipped with the latest electronic audio and video equipment for work and pleasure. It was a house of many surprises.

Some purists were unhappy that the finished minka did not more closely resemble the Gifu or Fukui originals. If it had, it would have been buttoned up against the snow, its small windows keeping out the light. In the perpetual summer of Hawaii, Yochan decided that something lighter and airier was demanded.

The champagne flowed and the stars, as they often do in Honolulu, brightened the night sky at Rusty's housewarming. Moving through the spotlighted house and gardens, the guests marveled at what they saw. Building a house can be maddening, exhausting, and finally exhilarating. Perhaps because it was three times as big as the norm, Rusty's magnified these emotions several times over.

A month after Yochan got his last payment and headed home, Rusty's world came apart.

In the late 1980s a sensational scandal broke around Wedtech, a South Bronx iron works company that President Ronald Regan had publicly praised for hiring hundreds of workers in a depressed time and area.

By the time it went through the courts, more than twenty local, state, and federal officials had been convicted of various charges of fraud, money laundering, racketeering, influence peddling, and other crimes.

Rusty, a friend and later partner of Wedtech's vice president, was accused and convicted of receiving an exorbitant fee for his services, a charge he indignantly denied. He told me he had earned it by advising the company how to enlarge and become more efficient. I believed him.

Fighting these accusations was a long and costly business. Lawyers' fees were steep. Rusty put the minka on the market less than a year after Yochan had built it. It was some consolation that he got nearly twice what he had paid for it. He later appealed to the U.S. Supreme Court, which overturned his conviction and some of the earlier ones. He was free.

Architectural Digest did a story and six-page color layout on the minka and its bayside complex. It was Yochan's third appearance in this distinguished American magazine. My minka was featured in the first, and another, erected in Karuizawa near Ernie Salomon's for the American wife of a Japanese businessman, was the second.

Without realizing it, Rusty did me an enormous favor when he commissioned Yochan to build the Honolulu minka. With the fee from that project, he and Reiko acquired an apartment on the edge of Waikiki. I had toyed with the idea of dividing my time between Kamakura and the United States after I retired in 1984; the new apartment, overlooking the sea and Diamond Head, has allowed me to do just that, as well as make annual visits to friends in San Francisco, Seattle, Los Angeles, New York, Boston, Maine, London, Paris, and Vilnius in Lithuania.

It had been a hectic, exhausting, and demanding time for Yochan and Reiko. A *Wall Street Journal* correspondent, interviewing them for a front-page feature story, asked what he had learned from the experience.

Yochan replied that he would sell and rebuild future minkas "in a much more businesslike way."

Then he added: "But I learned a lot about life."

Reiko, recalling the cockroaches and the thousands of meals cooked in a hot kitchen, exclaimed, "And I paid the tuition."

The East Gallery

Beginning in 1975 with Ernie Salomon's house, Yochan turned out one or two minkas a year until 1986. That was the year of the Rusty London adventure in Honolulu. Incredibly, he did two others in Japan in that twelve-month period, one for a printer in Zushi, next to Kamakura, and the other for a prune importer in the Hakone Lake area near Mt. Fuji. The young printer was so enamored of minkas after visiting mine that he tore down the large, modern house he had built only a few years before to make room for it.

Yochan's next burst of creativity took place in 1988 when he built a villa for a Swiss bank on Lake Yamanaka, in the shadow of Mt. Fuji, made an addition to my minka, and put up what he called the East Gallery of the House of Antiques, fifty yards away.

I never ceased to be astonished by the extraordinary energy and single-mindedness Yochan applied to these projects. It was even more remarkable that he accomplished as much as he did. Except for the Honolulu job, he generally relied on less than a handful of Shirotori carpenters. They had trucks and cranes and other mechanical aids, which were absent in building my house. And they no longer relied on a single, centuries-old shingle to guide them in the building process. A retired Kamakura architect and Yochan's elder brother did the many blueprints for the saunas, garages, and other new buildings demanded by customers far wealthier than I. But that was all the help he had.

Yochan often compares his minkas to large antiques, and if one considers the age and uniqueness of the posts and beams that are part of them, he is right. He is able to do so many in a year—it takes that long to build a single, modern Japanese house—because he is highly mobile and the original structure of a minka basically is prefabricated. It is quickly hammered together. The additions and variations are time consuming.

Yochan's pride in, and affection for, these old reminders of his boyhood drives him to take a much more active part in their reconstruction than most contractors or architects would. When one is going up he is either on the scene for days or commuting between Kamakura and the site almost daily.

The living room and all six bedrooms in the Swiss bank villa on the shore of Lake Yamanaka look out on Japan's national treasure, Mt. Fuji. It is a view most hotel owners would kill for. Yochan said in many ways it was almost pure minka, a pleasure to build.

Since their marriage in 1983, Yochan and Reiko had lived on the third floor of the West Gallery, leaving me in splendid isolation, but only for sleeping purposes. They joined me morning, noon, and night for meals around the large Danish table in the enlarged kitchen, or on more formal occasions at my round, painted Chinese table in the living room.

Though we lived in immense minkas, we were cramped for living space. This was not something they could complain about to visitors from Tokyo, who, unless they were very rich or on company expenses, paid exorbitant rent for inadequately small apartments.

Everyday life in the Japanese countryside is an open book. Everyone knows about everyone else because few if any have the luxury of privacy, a room of one's own. Minkas are built to accommodate many rice farmers and their families in the open, on futon mattresses spread out on the straw-matted tatami. One cannot close a door and shut out anyone else. For most rural Japanese, this is the normal state of affairs. Until recently, most people in the country lived and slept communally.

Before his marriage, Yochan slept on the second floor of my minka, under the eaves. The West Gallery apartment he and Reiko moved into proved small and inconvenient. They had to go down two flights to the bath.

My bedroom next door had a small garden and a splendid view beyond. But the proliferation of books, magazines, and newspapers made moving around it dangerous; I often slipped and nearly fell on them. Though this was not a fatal drawback, I was nonetheless thrilled when Yochan announced he wanted to build an annex, or as he called it, a Gate House, to the Nomura minka.

Work began with excavation of tons of dirt to make room for a ferroconcrete four-car garage, the same dirt that went into the landscaping of the third and final phase of my garden. On the solid foundation of the garage, Yochan built a three-story house entirely of new wood, which contained two spacious apartments, one on the first floor for him and Reiko, the other on the second floor for me.

Yochan seemed to delight in astonishing me. He had done so with the original Nomura minka and now he did so again with this new architectural achievement. I had been in Europe during most of the construction and thought Yochan intended to make the annex a modern structure. In the sense that each apartment had a bath, separate toilet, central heating and air-cooling, a small kitchen, and state-of-the-art laundry machine, which washed and dried by itself, it was. But the house, in its style and construction, owed almost as much to the eighteenth century as it did to the twentieth. Entirely of American pine—Yochan couldn't say, but

I hoped it was from Maine, the Pine Tree State—Yochan built it in the tongue-and-groove, or mortise-and-tenon style of the Nomura minka. He had bought the American timbers from his lumber dealer because he could find no Japanese ones long enough and straight enough for his purposes.

Unlike my minka, the roof beams met over an enormous eighteen-inch-thick, twelve-meter-long beam that ran the length of the house. It was a ridgepole to end all ridgepoles. On an earlier visit to Shirotori, a favorite Takishita uncle known for his calligraphy had signed the date and place on it. Always the poet, I wrote: "This stately 120-year-old pine bridges two cultures, Japanese and American." I signed my name, Waterville, Maine, and Shirotori, Japan.

I had indeed begun to think of myself as citizen of these two small cities, a bridge between them. Kamakura, old and historic, now witness to both the Heike and Minamoto eras through my minka, was the halfway mark between my love for America and Japan. What would the Florida man who had slammed me for being too sympathetic to the Hiroshima bomb victims have thought of this muddle in my loyalties? "Go home, you punk," he would have said. "Remember Pearl Harbor." But I was hooked. I could no more stop feeling that I belonged in both, such different places than I could have stopped breathing.

The Japan of today is not the hated Japan of Pearl Harbor. By a quirk of history—the 1949 conquest of China by Mao Tse-tung and his communists gained it American support—it is a vital American ally, democratic rather than militaristic, an economic partner, a friend with whom one occasionally disagrees, rather than an enemy. Some Americans relive the war and Pearl Harbor while refusing to acknowledge the cruelty of the atomic destruction of Hiroshima and Nagasaki. But I believe there is no profit in picking over old sores, fighting the war all over again. The present is the reality, not the past.

The Gate House differed in many respects from my minka, but it captured the mood. All the beams were large and straight; none had the glossy patina of age that centuries of smoky irori had given to mine. Because they were new and hewn from American pine, a bit of the sap still clung to them. They gave off a reddish-brown light, which made me think of log cabins in Maine. Then it came to me: the new pillars and beams of the Nomura minka must have looked like that in 1734. I had become used to thinking of all minkas as mahogany-colored just as art lovers forget the fact that all ancient Greek statues originally were painted in garish colors.

The Gifu carpenters put up the Gate House as they had the minka, with large wooden mallets, new and old tools. For Yochan it was a celebration of his years as a rescuer and renovator of old minkas. He was almost penniless when he supervised the erection of my minka, but like all the Takishitas, he was profligate with his time, strength, and dedication. Now, in building this new space for himself, Reiko, and me, he shouldered all the burden, physical, mental, and financial. I contributed nothing but encouragement and applause. In the early years when Yochan was going through college and getting started on his career, I had been there. Yochan, imbued with a filial devotion increasingly rare in modern Japan, never stopped repaying me. I was embarrassed. He felt he had not been all that generous.

My minka lay on an east-west axis, my bedroom and the living room facing out to the sea. Yochan joined the Gate House to it at right angles. In a sense, it crossed the T. Its roof was as steep as the original, to which it was attached. A perfectionist, Yochan tore off the black slate of my minka and installed new slate for both houses. This permitted the two houses to blend together so that they looked like one. To make the illusion even more complete, Yochan matched the plaster and wood. It was difficult after this to tell the difference between the new annex and the two-centuries-old original.

I believed myself fortunate to live on a Japanese hilltop overlooking the sea, came home from the office each day with eager anticipation. But some of my neighbors, forgetting or unaware that I had saved a national treasure, resented the fact that I lived in such a large house, even though it was a country minka. Not long after the Gate House was finished, I found at least one of them refused to share in the general approval. This critic complained about its height.

"I feel oppressed by it as I walk by," he or she told the Kamakura city government. I never learned the complainant's identity but soon heard from the architectural office, which sternly pointed out that Kamakura only allowed two-story residences. Yochan attended numerous meetings during which he explained that my minka was a cultural asset and would look grotesque if the Gate House roof, to which it was attached, were lower. I added to his entreaties, pointing out that in 1967 when my minka was built, there were no height limits. A half dozen experts came up the hill to see, and ended up complimenting me on the environmentally correct profusion of trees and bushes we had planted. There were suitable apologies, always de rigueur in these cases. Yochan boarded up the offending third-floor window, and the crisis passed.

Yochan had long eyed a piece of land at the entrance to the nearby park as a possible site for his projected East Gallery. Business was good and once more, as he had when working out of my minka, he felt the need to expand. This new gallery would allow him to exhibit his rapidly growing collection of framed paintings and particularly the colored and blue-and-white porcelains piled up in the West Gallery.

The land had lain unoccupied for years because no one could build on it. It was agreeably flat and ten feet from the road, but there was a precipitous drop after that. Once he had bought it, he faced a dilemma: fill the empty space with dirt, stones, and rubble to make it all flat, or build the gallery over it on reinforced concrete pillars. He chose the latter.

Though his love affair with minkas was undiminished, his experience with the Gate House gave him pause. The steep snow roof he envisioned would put it slightly higher than the limit. A painter living on a hill 500 yards away vowed to act if he exceeded it by a jot or a tittle. She feared her view of the distant sea would be blocked if he did.

What to do?

Yochan's solution: a white, American colonial-style house with a flat roof, spacious windows, and a pillared porch. Regulation height. Open the front door and the surprises begin. The visitor steps into the living room of a snow-country minka, with a set of beams and posts more complicated than mine. It has a raised tatami area, a chest-high fireplace, and a profusion of Chinese and Japanese art objects. In recent years a wide veranda on the north makes sitting under the trees a joy.

Steep stairs lead to the second floor and Yochan's many porcelains in glass display cases. The style is modern. Similar stairs down to the large basement reveal another western room, its beams covered by wood sheathing. This is where he displays his paintings, one of them a floor-to-ceiling scroll of a famous, long-dead sumo wrestler.

The painter keeps a sharp watch but finds nothing untoward to report.

Poppy and the Queens

The consequences of what one does are seldom anticipated. As the Nomura family of Ise in Fukui prefecture dedicated their new minka in the summer of 1734, they could not in their wildest imaginings guess what would happen to it 233 years later.

During those two and a fraction centuries, it faithfully served its original function as shelter for generations of Heike descendants: rice farmers, village, political, and religious leaders.

The rhythms of life rotated around the rice fields where men and women planted the seeds, waded hip-high in the muddy water to transplant the young shoots, and returned once more to gather in the harvest. It was a hard, cold, backbreaking existence, broken only by religious festivals, weddings, births, and funerals. For much of the year the Ise farmers were prisoners in their own homes, held there by heavy blankets of snow, which sometimes reached twenty feet in depth. The only escape was through a top-floor window, on snowshoes.

This was the situation, unchanged and unchanging in 1965 when I bought the Nomura minka. I had acquired it because of idle talk at breakfast and the indomitable determination of the Takishitas. Something more fundamental had forced the Nomuras to give up their ancestral home to a stranger: a foreigner, an American. It was progress, in the form of the second largest earth-fill dam in the world. They gave it up exactly 777 years after their Heike warrior ancestor had fled to safety from the victors of a distant and now long-forgotten battle.

The 1734 Nomuras would have scratched their heads in puzzlement if they had been told an American journalist would inherit it. In 1734 there was no United States.

They would have been equally confused to learn that the new owner would take it down, move it to Kamakura, the capital of their hated enemy, and do nothing but live in it. Where were the farmers, the rice fields, the bountiful harvests? There were none. That it would be warmed by oil, lit by electricity, and serviced by running water would tax credulity. Indoor toilets and baths? Impossible. The recorded music of Mozart? He wouldn't be born for another twenty-two years.

What would have astonished them most, perhaps, were the people who, in the next three decades of its existence in Kamakura, would come to praise and admire what they had created as a matter of course. It was said that the emperor, or the shogun, or anyway, someone high up, had spent the night in the Nomura minka. No one knew if, when, or why. The story was in the George Washington mode; the number of American homes in which it was said he slept suggested he did nothing but sleep all his mature life.

One of the earliest visitors of consequence, George H. W. Bush, would later become president of those same United States. He was then en route to China to be the official representative to the communist regime I knew so well. A mutual friend, Col. Joy Dow of Kennebunkport, Maine, wrote that the fledgling envoy should see me when he got to Tokyo.

Dutifully, Bush phoned and asked if he could come to Kamakura for a debriefing on China. He could and did, arriving with his wife Barbara, the American ambassador James Hodgson, and his wife, after taking half an hour to negotiate the sharp curves to the Great Peak in the embassy's stretch limousine. It normally takes three minutes. As president, he would never have been allowed by the Secret Service to do it. The road, narrow and twisting, is a certifiable security nightmare.

Over tea and cakes, Yochan and I entertained the Bushes for two and a half hours. The future president was a good listener, asked all the right questions. On a personal level, I, an ardent Democrat, found common ground in our friendship with Col. Dow and the Bushes' love of Kennebunkport, which I, and later Yochan, had visited.

Barbara, it turned out, didn't know Dow, steward of the Kennebunkport River Club, who knew George as "Poppy" when he was growing up.

"Can you tell me," she whispered to Roy Essoyan, my AP boss who was also present with his wife Betsey, "why we are here?"

Since the talk was almost entirely about China and my association with Mao and the other Red leaders, it seemed so obvious, he didn't reply.

I saw Bush again, in Peking, during the 1975 visit of President Gerald Ford. They posed for a photo, then Bush pulled Ford aside to tell him what a remarkable house I lived in.

Richard Nixon, another man who would become president, also called me in 1968 for a China debriefing. He didn't offer to go to Kamakura, instead asked that I appear at the American embassy, where he briefly welcomed me and turned me over to his chief aide and speech writer, Ray Price, an old *Herald Tribune* acquaintance of mine. It lasted two hours, and I like to think it contributed to Nixon's much applauded decision to establish diplomatic relations with a long-hostile Red China.

Of the many prominent and unusual people who came to the Great Peak, some writers, diplomats, journalists were my guests, but most wanted to meet Yochan and take a look at the Japanese and Chinese art he had accumulated. The real attractions, however, were my minka and Yochan's East and West galleries. Foreign visitors who saw the sights in Tokyo might buy pearls at Mikimoto, see the kabuki, visit a staggering assortment of museums and galleries, and do the astonishing department store scene. But Japanese folk houses were not on anyone's list for the simple reason that none were ordinarily available. By visiting Yochan or me, they would have the double pleasure of seeing one of these rare examples of Japanese architecture and doing some interesting browsing as well.

Many Japanese, like some gaijin, came only to look and not to buy. Sometimes they arrived in busloads, drank Reiko's tea, and left. But they told their friends, and many of them took their place.

Ambassadors and embassies marked the Great Peak down as something for their visitors to see. As a result, Yochan, Reiko, and I received a succession of cabinet ministers, state governors, minor royalty, and assorted other beneficiaries of the public purse. There also were artists, writers, journalists, musicians, orchestra conductors, movie actors, and directors whose intelligence and wit made their visits stimulating and memorable.

One of the more interesting people in this broad category was one who got away. Japan in 1980 awaited with anticipation Paul McCartney of the Beatles after a seven-year absence. Millions of tickets had been sold. The advance publicity was a drumroll reaching its crescendo. Our friends Dr. Tanaka and his wife Ingrid had been approached by his agent to find a suitable house for Paul's wife and children during the tour. Yochan agreed to rent them the West Gallery. From Peking, re-opening the AP's office after a thirty-year hiatus, I cautioned Japanese fans might tear the gallery apart for souvenirs. I needn't have worried. On his previous visit, McCartney had been warned for possessing a small amount of marijuana. Incredibly, it happened again, but this time he went to jail, was expelled, and the tour cancelled.

Both Yochan and I shared in the disappointment. Eager Beatles fans, we had hoped to meet him and his family on the Great Peak.

Dr. Tanaka and Ingrid brought many Scandinavians to our minka, including various Danish ambassadors. One day, the Danish embassy called to ask whether the dowager queen of Denmark and her daughter, the ex-queen of Greece, could see Yochan's collection.

They arrived from Tokyo in a minibus so small it had no difficulty negotiating the Great Peak curves. There were no guards, no policemen, no embassy attachés. The two women, one old, fragile, and courteously regal, the other still young and beautiful, yet modest, could not have been more genuinely natural and unassuming.

Yochan was impressed by the queen mother's knowledge of Japanese art. I recalled that she was an avid collector, a regular patroness of a Copenhagen antique shop owned by two of my friends.

Reiko poured tea and served cakes while Yochan and the queen talked knowledgeably of Imari porcelain and Japanese screens, one of which she bought. She left behind a Royal Danish porcelain piece as a souvenir of her visit.

When they had gone, I remarked on how truly democratic were the countries of Scandinavia and their leaders compared to the United States. No one of such stature would have traveled as freely, without bodyguards, as these two queens did.

It was an observation Yochan and Reiko remembered wryly after the 1993 visit of the American equivalent of royalty, First Lady Hillary Clinton.

Hillary and the Abbot

In April 1993, a plainclothes policeman from the Kamakura Police Department called on Yochan and Reiko. I was away in Honolulu.

"In July the United States and Japan will hold a summit meeting in Tokyo," he told them. "A big shot may be coming to Kamakura during that time. Your house is one of several places being considered for a visit. We'll call you later."

What then followed was a never-ending series of visits to the minka by local, prefectural, and national police, and finally the Secret Service from the White House.

About a week before the visit, White House and Japanese police met in my garage with Robin Berrington, the embassy officer assigned to the Hillary tour. While Reiko and Robin stood in the background, there ensued a loud and sometimes bitter exchange between the Secret Service and the Japanese. They debated over who should enter the minka. The Americans said they would take over, the Japanese could leave.

"We are responsible for the security of important visitors!" their leader shouted. "You are forgetting something. This is Japan."

The Secret Service backed down, and all twelve trooped into my living room. There the Americans, given tea by Reiko, apologized to the Japanese and the two undertook a final check. They then discussed where to put people during the visit.

Throughout all this, Reiko, a lady of great poise and patience, waited to ask a single question. During a pause in the talk she asked it.

"Can you tell me," she said, "whether Mrs. Clinton is actually coming or not?"

Incredibly, from April until July, with all the comings and goings and though all the signs pointed to it, neither she nor Yochan had been told, officially or unofficially, this bit of essential information.

Robin and the White House people looked surprised.

"Why, yes, of course," was the reply.

"Then is it to be lunch or tea?" she asked.

Told it would be lunch, she asked the inevitable next question: "How many?"

Robin counted on his fingers. "Seven, including yourselves," he said.

It could have been eight. In Honolulu, urged to join the party, I declined on the grounds that Reiko and Yochan had suffered through all the confusion and it should be their show. It cost me a lot to say so. A life-long Democrat and admirer of both Bill and Hillary Clinton, I would have given my eyeteeth to be there. I still marvel at my unaccustomed selflessness.

The White House people asked Reiko what she planned to serve. Robin, sensing her embarrassment—there were so many Hillary taboos—told them not to worry, he and she would work it out. He suggested cold chicken salad.

After he left, she thought about it.

"When one comes to lunch, you eat what the hostess serves," she reasoned. "I'll decide the menu myself: plenty of fruit and vegetables with chicken as the main dish."

She had the next day to do the shopping. Deciding she ought to be at table with her guests, she gave my maid, Tokumasa-san (admired successor to Suzuki of the Evil Eye) and Yochan's secretary, Matsumoto-san, a crash course in waiting on table, something they had never done outside their own families. They were told someone important was coming, but not who. They learned that the next day.

The Japanese foreign ministry knew all along and didn't like the fact that Hillary would be lunching with ordinary, non-diplomatic, non-governmental Japanese. In America, Jack Kennedy could dine with Ben Bradlee, editor of the *Washington Post*, after his election, but it just wasn't done in Japan. The embassy insisted.

"Do you think," I asked later, "the foreign ministry would have approved if I had been there?"

"Oh, no," said Reiko. "They wanted something stiff, formal, and uncomfortable. Also luxurious. After all, we were nobody and the minka didn't impress the foreign ministry people even though Americans loved it."

Twenty minutes after the scheduled hour, at noon, the guests arrived and quickly entered the garden under the eyes of Japanese and American security agents. A crowd of thirty or so neighbors, attracted by their presence, lined the dirt road.

They were Hillary; her mother Mrs. Rodham; the wife of the American ambassador Bonny Armacost; the wife of the Japanese ambassador to Washington, Mrs. Kuriyama; and Robin.

"After all the security checks," said Yochan, "it was something out of a James Bond movie. The ladies and Robin arrived in four standard autos and drove into the garage after the terrain had been scouted once again by the security people. The neighbors stood about wondering what was happening. They learned only later it was Hillary."

It was a hot summer day and everyone was dressed in cool cottons. Yochan and Reiko's instinct, as a matter of politeness when meeting someone so grand, was to dress to the nines, but since this was a private, informal affair, I suggested that they be casual. This added to the relaxed atmosphere.

Though the security people were everywhere they were invisible to the little group of luncheon guests. Two stood guard in a potato patch south of the minka. Reiko stocked the refrigerator in the West Gallery, where many of them were standing by, with food, soft drinks, and beer and invited them to help themselves.

Before they sat down to lunch around my 200-year-old lacquered Chinese table, Yochan took them on a tour of the minka, from the modern kitchen to the spacious, high-ceilinged second floor. Though she seemed to admire the huge beams and pillars, the thing that caught Hillary's eye was a gadget in the kitchen. Because in the past they had no cellars or refrigerators, in most minkas, food and vegetables were kept cool in a box suspended under the floor, called a *yukagura*. Lifting up the floor panel, Yochan revealed the contents of a modern-day yukagura: French wines.

"Mother, come see this," said Hillary, intrigued by its ingenuity.

From the beginning, Yochan, unaccountably shy, asked Reiko to do the talking (in English, there were no interpreters) but he soon found his tongue and dominated the Takishita side of the conversation.

"I was astonished at how relaxed Hillary was," he said later. "I expected her to be rather stiff, somewhat formidable."

At the table, he told her about the Japanese gulf between town and country and how things could be complicated when a country boy like himself married a sophisticated city girl with a samurai background like Reiko.

At this Hillary burst into loud laughter.

That summed up her relationship to Bill, she said. He was the country boy and she the sophisticated girl from Chicago. That was what she felt every time she visited his small hometown in Arkansas.

Reiko recalled that like most Japanese city girls, she had never been inside a minka before she met Yochan. What she saw then were the centrally heated, air-conditioned, transplanted, and renovated ones for which he was famous. After their marriage, he took her to Gifu and Fukui to see what they were like in the original: cold, dank, gloomy, and bug-infested.

The experience, she told Hillary, made her shudder at the thought she might have been asked to live in one of them.

Yochan was particularly taken by Hillary's mother, called her "mother" instead of Mrs. Rodham. She was visibly pleased by this.

Yochan and Reiko had agreed they would not talk politics or religion or any other potentially ticklish subject. But Hillary started off with questions about the Japanese election, which they answered at length.

Reiko began the lunch with cream of pumpkin soup followed by chicken breasts coated with her special sauce, wrapped in potato flakes, and baked in the oven. Asparagus and mounds of fresh fruit followed. There were no leftovers. Yochan dug up a bottle of premier cru French white wine from the yukagura, which Hillary didn't touch. The other guests were not so hesitant. She did, however, use salt in abundance.

After lunch, Yochan took the guests next door to his West Gallery and between showing some of his painted screens told them the history of the minka and my relationship to the

Takishitas. He gave her a copy of my book, *Covering China*, out only a few months earlier.

As they left, Yochan presented Hillary with an Imari porcelain plate and a gift from an unexpected source: the abbot of a thousand-year-old Shinto shrine in Chiba. Hillary gave them a Steuben glass vase.

The whole thing lasted two and a half hours and put Hillary behind schedule. She had to skip an appearance before waiting crowds in downtown Kamakura.

There were thirty Japanese and American security people for this very private lunch from which the press was barred. In the middle of the lunch, Reiko recalled, a package arrived addressed to her and Yochan. The security people took it gingerly into the tatami room next door and opened it, ready for any contingency. It contained pickles and noodles from Yochan's mother in the country.

Tomiya Takanashi, of the thirtieth generation of abbots of the Shinto Cherry Tree Shrine in Chiba prefecture, spread out the Tokyo newspaper. A slender man in his mid-forties, he was scheduled to preside over the groundbreaking for a new house and was wrapping the green branches of the sacred sakaki tree he would need for the ceremony. In doing so, his eye fell on an article in the paper about Yochan and his career as a restorer of minkas. Since his parents' thatch-roofed minka had begun to tilt alarmingly, he noted Yochan's phone number, finished wrapping the branches, and quickly left.

Descendant of a distinguished Tokyo family, he had elected to enter the Shinto priesthood. At the seminary he met and fell in love with a gentle and strikingly beautiful fellow-student from the

family that, in addition to producing Kikkoman soy sauce
and wines, owned the ancient Cherry Tree (Sakuragi) Shrine.
When they married, he not only took his wife's family name but
inherited the shrine. All that remained of the once imposing main
structure, however, was a tiny wooden affair, little more than a
reminder of the glory that it had once been.

The Takanashis, now both Shinto priests, planned to restore
the Cherry Tree Shrine to its old grandeur. They had already made
a profitable sale of the shrine land and owned a large wooded tract
nearby, on which they intended to build. A guesthouse for the
faithful would be the first building of the new complex. The article
on Yochan had given Tomiya an idea. He picked up the phone and
called Kamakura. Would Yochan be willing to look at his parents'
house? He would.

During the repairs, which Yochan and his crew made,
the Takanashis watched him closely. He was about their age and
shared their enthusiasms. They liked his style and personality.
They became friends. When he had finished, they asked him
about the guesthouse. How did he envision it?

A few weeks later, Yochan sketched out his concept in
words and on paper. He proposed an H-shaped, one-story
wooden building that would contain a sleeping area for up to a
hundred pilgrims, a central office for shrine business, and a large
public space for tea and meals. The entire building, with an all-
copper roof, would be bigger and more unusual than any he had
undertaken. It combined the rough-hewn honesty and integrity of a
mountain minka with the elegantly simple wooden architecture of
a typical Shinto shrine. To this he boldly added a mix of Victorian
fixtures and modern heating and plumbing.

The Takanashis were thrilled. They asked him to proceed as soon as possible.

But during the digging of the foundation, the laborers unearthed a treasure trove of artifacts from the Yayoi period, between 300 BC and 300 AD. The site apparently had been a rich cultural center. Hundreds of clay pots and dishes, some intact, others only shards, came to light. The find created a sensation in archeological circles. It also put the guesthouse project on hold for a year while the Ministry of Education's experts went over the area with the archeological equivalent of a fine-toothed comb. Part of the treasure went to the shrine, part to national museums. All the pieces were carefully photographed.

In the years since Ernie Salomon's wife had implored her husband to buy her a minka for her birthday, Yochan concentrated only on residences, with one exception, a teahouse for the once-great Jyomyoji Buddhist Monastery in Kamakura for which he supplied the design but not the construction. It was an architectural jewel, one deserving of a place in any textbook. That design in the classical temple style gave him a small foretaste of what was required for the guesthouse of the reborn Sakuragi Shrine in Chiba.

It posed an interesting challenge, something between the sacred and the profane. The shrine itself, which would be built later, had to conform to the strictest standards of Shinto architecture, one of the oldest known to humans. But the guesthouse, catering to pilgrims and the faithful, had greater leeway. It was not a sacred structure.

Yochan's concept was one of simplicity combined with sophistication, of man in communion with the gods of nature, and man in real life. It was a daring idea, one that could have gone wrong, but it succeeded admirably.

The most striking feature from the outside was the copper roof, a vast expanse, which over the years would provide incomparable protection and with age and weather, the blue-green patina found in ancient bronzes.

The raising of the roof was marked by a celebration medieval in its splendor. The abbot did not stint. He dressed himself, Yochan, and the builders in replicas of the multicolored silk blouses, pantaloons, and black lacquered hats of his Shinto ancestors. They mingled with a crowd of several hundred guests then, to the wailing of flutes and the beating of drums, mounted the roof and posed beside large bundles of straw-wrapped rice donated by the devout. The ceremonies that followed were similar to those for the roof raising of my house, except that they were longer, grander, and more impressive. Afterward, the abbot and abbess served dinner and sake to the assembled guests.

"It was one of the most thrilling moments of my life," Yochan said. "For years I had studied and admired the paintings of the Heian period from a distance, as it were. To be dressed like that and take part in a serious, ancient ceremony recalling that time is exciting. It takes you back, way back."

Yochan completed the guesthouse a week before Hillary and her mother came to lunch in my minka. Widely traveled and intelligent, the Takanashis admired the Clintons, Hillary in particular. When Yochan was about to leave Chiba, the abbot gave him a neatly wrapped package.

"Please give this to Mrs. Clinton," he said, "as a token of our respect and admiration."

Inside was a rare silk replica of a tenth-century prioress robe, which Yochan presented to her after lunch.

I also benefited from the abbot's generosity. On my first visit to the completed guesthouse, I met and talked at length with him, spoke of the Greek gods and their relationship to nature, and of my own admiration of modern-day Shinto and its belief in the powers of nature. My knowledge may not have been deep, but I conveyed it with enthusiasm. In a short time, we became friends.

As I left with Yochan and Reiko, the abbot pressed into my hands a bundle hastily wrapped in newspaper.

"A souvenir of your visit," he said.

It was a 2000-year-old Yayoi period clay sake cup, one of those unearthed at the shrine before Yochan began work.

Linking East and West, old and new, Japanese and American, it sits in an honored place in my old minka.

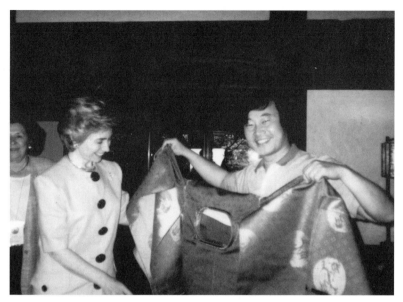

Yochan presents Hillary with a replica of a tenth-century Shinto prioress's gown.

Epilogue

The Japanese endured long and bitter life under eight hundred years of feudalism. Before becoming a modern nation in 1868, they were under the often-cruel rule of military dictators, shoguns. The common herd had to obey the shoguns' military retainers, samurai, totally and unhesitatingly. Those who resisted lost their heads, immediately and without trial. These habits of centuries made the samurai class unbeatable warriors and the rest of the population among the most docile on earth.

Formed over such a long period, this kind of blind subservience is hard to break. During the fierce battles of the Pacific war, Japanese soldiers demonstrated, probably for the last time, unquestioning loyalty and obedience to the emperor. Ordered to fight to the finish, they died by the thousands rather than surrender.

Japan cut itself off from the rest of the world from 1616 to 1868 and imprisoned, tortured, or executed thousands of Christians suspected of being the vanguard of a foreign invasion. These Christians, both foreign and native, were the object of official persecution, which lasted for more than two hundred years. This deeply rooted anti-foreignism persisted throughout the Pacific war in examples of cruelty and torture toward American and European prisoners of war.

Ironically, it was American policy carried out by the American military occupation that changed long-held hostile Japanese attitudes and made it a success.

The U.S. administration under Harry Truman had a choice. It could impose a hard and cruel peace, as the Japanese themselves had on those they had conquered. Memories of Japanese atrocities still kindled feelings of hate in most Americans; some in positions of power in Washington urged that Japan be reduced to the status of a fourth-rate agricultural society, forever unable to threaten anyone again.

Or it could astonish everyone, including the Japanese, by adopting a policy of tolerance, compassion, and enlightenment toward the defeated nation: what a later generation would call "tough love."

Prodded by New Deal liberals and faced with the threat of the Soviet Union and the newly created People's Republic of China, Truman chose the carrot rather than the stick.

It was an undertaking like no other in history. Under the driving force of General Douglas MacArthur, Japan completed its long and tortured march from feudalism and imperial rule to complete democracy. Women were given the vote; land was redistributed; the big *zaibatsu*, industrial monopolies, dissolved; and human rights written into law. The capstone in this new and extraordinary structure was the American-inspired constitution, whose article nine forbade Japan from ever waging war again as a means of advancing its foreign policy.

The Japanese, weary, like Katoji, of war and bloodshed, embraced the occupation reforms, including the no-war constitution, with fervor.

Today, though it is the second most powerful country economically on earth, it does not possess a nuclear bomb. Its military forces are committed only to self-defense. In the years since its crushing defeat, it is a nation at peace with itself and its neighbors. It has threatened or attacked no other country, taken part in none of the numerous wars which have since wracked the globe.

The Takishitas are proud that Japan, alone among the great powers, has kept the peace for so many years. But there are some extremists who yearn to revise the no-war constitution and acquire a nuclear arsenal.

Their maneuverings are warily watched and criticized by the large majority, who believe war is not the best means of resolving international disputes.

Yochan is one of them.

In 2007, he continues the brilliant architectural career he began when he built my minka in 1967.

In 1999, he acquired the old Tanaka house, whose hated fence gave us such heartaches, and replaced it with an architectural jewel, a three-story city minka called a *sukiya*. Its concealed beams, varied wooden interior, tatami flooring, and clean, spare design meets the definition of shibui, restrained elegance.

After completing it, he took time off and, with Reiko's help and some unneeded advice from me, produced a beautiful book of photographs of sixteen of his minkas.

Entitled *Japanese Country Style* and published by Kodansha International, it is a visually stunning work in English and Japanese, whose text and images illustrate his success in making these old farmhouses livable and loveable.

The book is dedicated to me, his mother, and his father.

Seven years ago, Katoji, always energetic, began to feel physically weak. He was eighty-seven and recognized his approaching death. It was poignant testimony to the affection he felt for me, and the house he had built for me, that he chose to spend his last hours in the sunny room that had been my bedroom for twenty years.

Tended faithfully by Reiko and Yochan and surrounded by his family, the end came peacefully a few months later. Hundreds of his fellow townspeople turned out for his funeral in Shirotori. They admired him for his bravery as a soldier and a firefighter, his uncompromising devotion to the truth and what he believed right. That included his forthright friendship, unusual at the time, with me, and the other Americans who, in a grimmer day, had been his enemies.

After the Buddhist ceremonies, his ashes were deposited on the grounds of the mountain temple he had loved and supported all his life.

Later, through his tears, Yochan translated the Buddhist inscription on the front of the gravestone, then read the names Katoji had had engraved on the back, members of the family whose ashes would later be buried beside his.

Mine appeared at the bottom, after Yochan's.

(top) Kamakura and the sea beyond the finished east roof and dormer.
(bottom) Yochan sits on the porch outside the living room gazing at the sea.

(top) *Sitting in the old stable, I pass idle days in happy contentment.*

(bottom) *The baronial living room with its gold-lacquered Chinese table, at which Hillary dined.*

(top) Yochan in the garden with the minka he reconstructed.
(bottom) An architectural tone poem: my ancient minka dusted in snow.

Acknowledgments

Many people, too numerous to name, helped me understand the complexities of minka-building and at the same time gave me insights into the rural Japanese way of life. Without them this book would not have been possible.

My first and most valued teachers were the Takishitas of Shirotori, in the mountainous snow country of Gifu prefecture. Their youngest son, Yoshihiro, a distinguished minka architect himself, encouraged me to write of my experiences.

The Associated Press showed me what was possible by printing an article in *AP World*, its house organ, entitled "The House That Love Built." This was followed three years ago by a widely circulated story about my minka and its meaning to me.

Norm Goldstein, AP's book and features editor, read the manuscript and made valuable suggestions. Prof. Tom Hilgers of the University of Hawaii arranged to digitize it. Nancy Eklund Later, acquisitions editor of Princeton Architectural Press, enthusiastically recommended it for publication.

In the publishing process, my editor, Dorothy Ball, took a manuscript that rambled and sometimes got lost and, with patience and persistence, made it leaner and more concentrated. For this I owe her a writer's gratitude.

Shawn Dolley, an architect from my home town of Waterville, Maine, and Bill Feltz, cultural officer of the East-West Center, made it possible to move and edit the manuscript digitally between New York City and Honolulu.